The Essential Guide to
CONTEMPORARY DANCE TECHNIQUES

The Essential Guide to
CONTEMPORARY DANCE TECHNIQUES

MELANIE CLARKE

THE CROWOOD PRESS

First published in 2020 by
The Crowood Press Ltd
Ramsbury, Marlborough
Wiltshire SN8 2HR

enquiries@crowood.com

www.crowood.com

British Library Cataloguing-in-Publication Data
A catalogue record for this book is available from the British Library.

ISBN 978 1 78500 699 9

Frontispiece: Cunningham class featuring dancers Alice Lebant and Valeria Famularo; Trinity Laban Conservatoire of Music and Dance. Copyright James Keates.

Designed and typeset by Guy Croton Publishing Services, West Malling, Kent

Printed in India by Replika Press Pvt Ltd

CONTENTS

DEDICATION

For J and E: you can achieve whatever you work for.

ACKNOWLEDGEMENTS

There are many contributors to this book whom I would like to thank: firstly, dance technique teachers working in high profile institutions have shared their practices to provide an insight into approaches to teaching and learning, as well as identifying what they consider to be essential features of contemporary dance techniques. All these contributors explore their practice from the perspective of teaching on Higher Education programmes in contemporary dance, and willingly entered into dialogue about their practices; more detailed biographical notes about them may be found in Appendix II.

I would also like to thank the following: the photographer, James Keates, who brought his expertise and open willingness to photograph real technique classes to produce images for this book. The dancers who participated in the photographed classes. Helen Thomas for sound advice, feedback and encouragement. Ruth Clarke and Tyrone Duff for constant support and belief in me (I could not have done any of this without you). In memory of my father, N. Clarke, who was a performer, and my grandfather, W.H.R. Evans, who was a teacher.

ABOUT THE AUTHOR

Melanie Clarke grew up in Stockport with parents who were both performers. She studied Musical Theatre at North Cheshire Theatre School from the age of four to eighteen. Her mum says that she did her first dance class at three but didn't like it; however, at the age of four she asked to go back, and she hasn't stopped to this day. She discovered Contemporary Dance at fourteen, and at eighteen started the BA Hons Dance Theatre at Trinity Laban Conservatoire for Music and Dance (then the Laban Centre). Two years after graduating she returned to Trinity Laban to take on a Graduate Internship, and the year after joined the faculty whilst completing her Masters in Dance Studies, which included Dance Documentation and Reconstruction, Dance in Education, and Choreography.

She works as an independent choreographer alongside her teaching, creating, performing and touring works as a solo artist and alongside her company, bluewhite. She has created and toured eleven original works, and choreographed commissions for TanzTheatre Giessen and Trinity Laban.

At Trinity Laban she is currently Programme Leader for the Dance Diploma Programmes. She is a Teaching Fellow of Trinity Laban and a Fellow of the Higher Education Academy. She teaches Release-based Technique and Choreological Studies, tutors students' research, and choreographs new work.

Fig. 1: Melanie Clarke. JAMES KEATES

She has presented conference papers on Labanotation and applications of Laban's theories. With Joukje Kolff she notated a score of Yvonne Rainer's seminal work *Trio A*, which is available to loan from the Dance Notation Bureau in New York. Melanie reconstructed *Trio A* on dancers for the 'Move Choreographing You' exhibition at the Hayward Gallery in 2010.

INTRODUCTION

In this book the essential features of learning the technical skills to prepare to work in the contemporary dance genre, and the routes and pathways that this learning process could take are identified and highlighted. This book is written from the perspective of the training dancer – what learning to dance through a particular style and technique of movement might be like. It is not aimed towards establishing a series of ideals that the dancer must conform to, but to support an understanding of the learning situation in the context of its development and approach. The intention is to allow access to the requirements of different technique practices, but also an insight into the purpose of these processes.

The three exemplars of technical practices presented here will be analysed for their learning potentialities. The aim is to reveal a practice in terms of its origins and purposes, and its subsequent development as a methodology for passing on dance skills. The three technique forms are Graham Technique, developed by Martha Graham; Cunningham Technique developed by Merce Cunningham; and Release-based Technique developed by many dancers and somatic practitioners. These have been chosen from the plethora of possibilities for their distinctiveness from each other, and for the span of time that separates their development, Graham Technique emerging from the 1930s, Cunningham from the 1940s and Release-based from the 1980s. All these techniques are still practised, or still influence practices in the twenty-first century.

New techniques are emerging from the development of dance as an art form, and from the developing range of possibilities for movement creation and performance influenced and emerging from dance heritage, popular culture, globalization, the new understanding of the body and other artistic practices.

The three techniques outlined in this book attempt to delineate aspects of contemporary dance heritage and changes in practice that influence current higher education teaching programmes. The myriad unnamed practices of individual teachers have developed from a heritage that exists in and around these three exemplars. By understanding the distinctiveness of these three practices, an understanding of contemporary dance technique can emerge. Exploring and analysing these approaches will open up a reflective capacity, which can be applied to all dance experiences.

My personal understanding of contemporary dance technique comes from my own dance training and subsequent twenty years of professional practice as a teacher, dancer, choreographer and movement analyst. As a teacher of contemporary dance technique in higher education, I have reflected on, and researched around my experiences and approaches, and have discussed such teaching with colleagues and visiting artists. My approach to discerning my own practices, and those of others, comes from my embodied 'knowing' as a dancer, inter-related to my knowledge of two practices developed from the pioneering work of twentieth-century choreographer, teacher and researcher, Rudolf Laban.

Laban was an active researcher into dance and human movement, and he instigated methodologies for exploring and illuminating dance as a practice; these are Labanotation (the symbol system first conceived by Rudolf Laban in 1922, and developed as a comprehensive framework for movement analysis and recording), and choreological studies (the field of analysis of the structures of human movement, and the application of these to dance performance). These two approaches create a framework for understanding and articulating movement in ways derived from dance, rather than other areas of analytical study. Labanotation and choreological studies provide a lens through which dance practice can be illuminated, and a language through which it can be articulated.

The structure of this book is an example of one of these approaches, as a choreological framework is used. This field of study utilized Laban's insight into the structures of human movement, to develop ways of understanding, analysing, exploring and creating dance as a performative act. The qualitative and intentional acts of movement emerge from the constants of the physics of the moving body within the environment of our world, but become embodied

acts of communicative and expressive potential. Part of the dancer's ability beyond the bio-mechanics of the body is the skill to select or manipulate movement to create a visual affect. This factor is what distinguishes dance from other physical activities, and allows for the title 'performance art'.

Art is a created act, it is something that is made, and made to be viewed. The performative nature of the dancer's skill means that achieving the physical requirements of the movement goes hand in hand with a performative approach, as dance is the integration of both. Using a choreological framework to view dance technique will highlight this relationship and integration, and make the discernment of the skill acquisition embodied in these practices accessible. Knowing what specific sets of skills are embodied in different practices can enable a clarity in what the dancer is trying to achieve and understand through them. The aim is to support the doing and knowing that comes from embodied learning.

CHAPTER 1

LEARNING CONTEMPORARY DANCE TECHNIQUE

THE EVOLUTION OF CONTEMPORARY DANCE

Contemporary dance is a broad and diverse art form despite its relatively short history. It arose in various parts of the world in the twentieth century as a liberation from the structures and aesthetic of ballet, as individuals searched for new forms of dance. As the body was freed from the corsets and morality of the nineteenth century, a more visceral and socially relevant theatrical performance became possible. Pioneers such as Ruth St Dennis and Ted Shawn, Rudolf Laban, Isadora Duncan and Loi Fuller worked to find new forms of theatrical expression, and instigated the foundations for a creative explosion in dance.

One hundred years later there is a wealth of avenues for movement exploration in terms of learning opportunities and creative possibilities. In the twenty-first century, individual expression, creativity and innovation are synonymous with contemporary dance as an art form. But what does that mean for the aspiring dancer? Dancing may be a spontaneous act of freedom of expression in everyone's life, but dance as an art form is a learnt and created act. Through educating ourselves in movement, we, as contemporary dancers, not only enable our movement possibilities to surpass the average, but we also develop our bodily awareness and understanding of movement.

Part of this learning is through contemporary technique classes, since, put very simply, learning a technique is learning a way to do things – providing yourself with the knowledge to be able to do something. But dance technique is not just one thing, but an array of approaches and methodologies akin to the array of artistic practices in contemporary dance. Dance technique is a physical learning process, and not only a bio-mechanical one. It is an experiential envelopment in a vast array of processes, practices, aesthetics and sensations.

LEARNING THROUGH EMBODIED PRACTICE

In contemporary dance educational programmes in the UK students usually do not study only one particular set of forms and structures – that is, one technique form – but have an experiential knowledge of diverse movement possibilities, and the particular application of these to diverse tasks and processes. Different schools, such as higher education conservatoires and university dance departments, approach this education in different ways. Many provide access to a range of techniques or a range of teachers with different backgrounds and approaches. Some programmes include supplementary training separate from what is called technique class, such as fitness classes, conditioning, Pilates, yoga, somatic practices, experiential anatomy. Improvization practices can be considered as technical training or as creative practice, or both.

Whatever the structural approach, as a dancer you have to discover yourself within the application of your bodily movement to the approaches presented to you. You need to learn, for example, how you can understand the sensations of your hip socket functioning, and how you use that *embodied* knowledge to move your legs and torso in particu-

Fig. 2: Release class taught by Zoi Dimitriou, featuring dancers Alice Lebant, Valeria Famularo and Carolina Ravaioli; Trinity Laban Conservatoire of Music and Dance, London. JAMES KEATES

lar ways in different practices, with different uses of energy in time and space for particular expressive or performative purposes that you generate or in which you find meaning. Not a simple task! It takes time and dedication to achieve this for every aspect of yourself as an integrated and performative whole. Although it can seem daunting at times, understanding what you are trying to achieve can help to make sense of the process of learning, and how you support yourself within it.

There are no direct pathways from learning one technical practice to performing within that style, so the contemporary dancer needs to be technically able, but also adaptable to current and future creative practices and performance modes in an open and ever-changing genre. The very open-endedness of contemporary dance as an artistic practice can actually throw into question what good contemporary dance technique even means, as it is not an end in itself. Current choreographic practices in contemporary dance utilize the performers' creativity through improvization and task-based movement creation, and so often embodied creative decision-making can be desired as much as physical facility and/or a particular movement skill set.

The requirement to be not only a strong technician, but also a creative practitioner implies the possibility to use what is learnt in creative ways. Learning technical skills should then not prevent creative choice, but should enable the dancer to physically achieve the creative vision (which often evolves from creative processes) of others (or themselves).

Thus, learnt movement skills need to be open, accessible to creative exploration, and this requires education into movement potentials and physical strategies rather than the simple ability to repeat movement patterns. In other words, the steps, and picking up steps, is not the aim. Remembering movement phrases is a useful skill in the learning process, but it is not the goal. The ultimate achievement is to acquire body management and performance skills through experience. Experiencing dance is to use all aspects of yourself: you use the physical abilities of your body, the abilities of your brain for pattern recognition, retaining concepts,

Fig. 3: Students in a Graham class taught by Geneviève Grady, featuring dancers Kirbie Franks and Jessy MacKay; Trinity Laban Conservatoire of Music and Dance, London. JAMES KEATES

reflecting on experiences and connecting ideas together, and you use your personal approach to expression and communication.

Knowledge and understanding comes from the integration of all these things within the experience of dancing. Dance practice is an embodied practice whereby you, as a whole person, are the thing you represent, the dance. What you gain in the practice

Fig. 4: Floor exercises in a technique class, featuring dancers Anna Broome, Pagan Hunt, Federica Bertani, Mitchell Davis, Laure Dubanet and Alice Lovrinic; Trinity Laban Conservatoire of Music and Dance, London. JAMES KEATES

of learning in, about and through dance is knowledge about yourself as a dancer, as well as dance as an activity and as an art form. The learning is not just the doing, but a reflection on how the dance is experienced to be produced by the dancer. You become the repository of all your learning and experience, and you can call on all, or any of that to facilitate your performative intention. In this way dance can be said to be an embodied practice.

DANCE TECHNIQUE

Dance technique teachers have a responsibility to enable an education in dance, as well as the acquisition of physical skills and abilities – but how to do that is not set in stone. There are many named approaches to learning contemporary dance technique. Various forms of technique were developed through the twentieth century by particular artists with particular creative visions. Initially these techni-cal forms were to establish an aesthetic basis for an individual's choreographic practice, but these forms are still widely utilized in dance training as methods for accessing dance skills. Then dance technique practices arose that used an approach to technique teaching that was not attached to a choreographic vision. In the twenty-first century all styles of tech-nical training are adapting to the demands of the profession in order to equip dancers with open technical skills and creative potentials.

Individual teachers have the possibility of developing a personal teaching approach, which means they do not have to teach as they were taught, but can themselves adapt and make choices to facilitate the learning of particular groups of individuals. Due to this professional freedom, dance technique forms are approached as a basis to teach from, rather than an imposed structure. Techniques are not historical records of previous choreographic styles, but working practices in the pursuit of dance skills. Given this variability on approach, student dancers are exposed to a range of practices and approaches. Experiencing differentiation in learning can support a dancer's adaptability and creative potential.

However, it can make learning dance a complex and potentially confusing process. The contemporary dancer does not just need to execute different steps, but must be open to different approaches to learning, different physical sensations, and different performance modes. Understanding the background and aesthetic basis of different forms, as well as the approach to learning and performing embedded in the basis of different forms of technical practice, can support the learner to make these adaptations and access the broad perspective of contemporary dance.

In this book three distinct approaches to learning contemporary dance will be discussed: Graham, Cunningham and Release-based techniques. There are many different forms and practices of dance technique developed by choreographers or by teachers as methods of enabling dancers to experience particular ways of moving, and to gain skills. There can be as many approaches as there are teachers teaching them, as there is no set form for what contemporary dance is, and thus no one way to learn it.

Some technical practices have been used for many years by influential choreographers and teachers such as Merce Cunningham, Martha Graham, Doris Humphrey, Jose Limon and Lester Horton, and their practices have become established as technique forms with designated names (usually the choreographer's surname). Other practices, such as Release-based technique, are various in appear-

Fig. 5: Dancer Anna Broome; Trinity Laban Conservatoire of Music and Dance, London.
JAMES KEATES

ance but bonded by a set of principles. There are also approaches that are an amalgamation of ideas and methods by individual teachers, or new and emerging technical styles such as Flying Low and Gaga Technique.

Individual teachers are generally free to choose what and how to teach, and so each individual teacher's approach can be distinct. Some follow a particular lineage and teach from a named perspective with a particular set of concerns, although how they go about teaching it will still be reliant on their personal experiences, and the context in which they relate to their students.

There is no syllabus for contemporary technique as there is for other dance forms, such as ballet and tap, through organizations such as The Royal Academy of Dancing (RAD) or the Imperial Society of Teachers of Dancing (ISTD). As previously stated, it is not a series of steps that you learn how to do. Rather, it is how you learn about how to achieve things with and through your own body. The goal is to enable and educate yourself in dancing. This can be a shift in thinking, as dance classes are not a place where you necessarily have to get it right. Instead it is a place where you can learn from mistakes, experiment, try different methods and approaches, and discover new things.

As you learn about yourself, as a mover, you start to realize the complexity of the resource you have; that is, yourself and the field of dance. Through the practice of technique class, you build awareness, and through this awareness you build skills, knowledge and values. You need to *reflect* (think deeply and carefully) on the process of learning and the sensorial experience of moving, and thus on your awareness of yourself as a learner and a dancer.

Reflective practice is about taking time to consider your experiences, and what you can glean from them; thinking about what has happened to you in your experiences and interactions with others may provide information about your learning preferences

Fig. 6: Working autonomously, featuring dancers Kirbie Franks and Anna Broome; Trinity Laban Conservatoire of Music and Dance, London. JAMES KEATES

Fig. 7: Feeling yourself moving: Release class taught by Melanie Clarke, featuring dancer Luca Braccia; Trinity Laban Conservatoire of Music and Dance, London. JAMES KEATES

and reactions. How do you manage challenges, how do you deal with frustration, when is it easy for you to focus and stay motivated, and when is it difficult? By cultivating a *self-reflective* awareness you can develop effective learning strategies using a range of different approaches. Self-reflective awareness can support you in developing your personal *autonomy* and in taking ownership of your learning.

Sometimes these reflective experiences can be called the 'toolbox' – a set of open possibilities that can be combined, re-ordered, mixed up, integrated, to fit the circumstances. Toolbox is a useful metaphor, although it can imply that the skills are something separate from you, which of course they are not – dance knowledge is you: once you learn something through embodied experience you are changed, as you now incorporate that knowing in who you are as a person. Being open to the possibility of changing is therefore essential for learning. Gaining your embodied knowledge is facilitated by teachers offering you explorations and experiences based on the free sharing of their knowledge.

Your discernment in recognizing and appreciating the offering of your learning opportunities is a motivation for this book. You cannot be taught how to be the dancer you are, but you can have the techniques revealed to you that can enable you to embody intention without hindrance. Technique class is a preparation for dancing and an opportunity to dance. It is where you can build the possibilities to let the dancing emerge from you – to create it and express it. Dance is a way of being, a method of self-expression, a personal empowerment. There is a term called *soma*, which is the lived, self-aware body, the integration of all that constitutes a person as a physical being. Dance is a method of meeting yourself as a self-aware physical being, and from that place you can develop, transform, learn and change through conscious practice.

Different dance forms and techniques have distinct styles and performance modes. Individuals may have preferences for particular ways of moving based on their character and personal idiosyncratic movement preferences. Thus, understanding the particular movement choices and performance functions of different techniques can reveal the approaches within a technique which can affect the feeling state in the body when they are executed; this is why individuals may prefer certain styles to others, or may be more challenged by certain styles than they are by others.

Technique classes are the means to learn how to achieve dance, and should never be an endless repetition of unachievable steps. It is a means of moving towards enabling you to be an individual, and thus is a process of discovery that involves the whole person in a personal journey; it is a *subjective* (personal) experience, as we are it. Learning means gaining new knowledge, so a learning process is about exposing ourselves to things we don't know, and gaining insight into them. This is very different from getting steps right. Aiming for accuracy is a good ambition, but correctness should not be the main, or only, criterion for success.

KNOWLEDGE AND COMMITMENT

One of the potential frustrations of learning dance technique is that you can't just do the movement you want to do. You may make an approximation of something based on the embodied knowledge you already have, but that means you are re-enacting what you already know, rather than developing new skills. To develop new skills you have to find a way into opening up and utilizing possible functions of the body that you are not yet aware of. This often relies on a process of discovery that can take you out of the comfort of what you know you know, as you have to rediscover yourself in new ways in order to do new things in your own body.

Your teacher can support that process through structuring a learning journey over time, building up embodied knowledge and skills in order to make particular movements possible to achieve. They can also provide insights from their own acquired knowledge in how *they* learnt to understand how to create movement with their body. Ultimately, however, it is the student who has to do the learning, as it can only be subjective knowledge. As Release Technique teacher (with an MSc in Dance Science) Tina

Krasevec says: 'It is really up to them in creating this, it is not up to me to create this: they are really creating this, and I am just trying to support that.'[1]

Talent needs to be nurtured and pursued to really exist. No one is born a professional dancer; they may show aptitude, but it is a strong dedication and motivation to learn that enables aptitude to become manifest as ability. Likewise, creativity does not spring out of nowhere: rather it is the ability to use knowledge and skills in interesting and new ways. To create dance there needs to be a conscious decision-making process, and that implies some knowledge on the part of the maker. The gaining

of knowledge takes focus and many hours of work; the deeper and more sophisticated the knowledge, the greater the choices and possibilities for the dancer. Learning processes take time – there is no quick route. A commitment to the process of learning over time is essential, so the motivation to learn must be strong.

Undertaking a focused, developmental approach to learning, facilitated by someone with greater knowledge, can be an efficient long-term process but can also feel somewhat removed from the ultimate goal. Understanding the need to build the foundations of movement knowledge, and refine the

LEFT: **Fig. 8: Working your body, featuring dancers Kirbie Franks and Alice Lovrinic; Trinity Laban Conservatoire of Music and Dance, London.**
JAMES KEATES

ABOVE: **Fig. 9: Positive learning environment, featuring dancers Alice Lovrinic and Rosemary Copp; Trinity Laban Conservatoire of Music and Dance, London.**
JAMES KEATES

skills that underpin successful execution of movement, can often be the biggest hurdle to overcome when starting to approach dance learning in professional training. This process can happen at any time of life. There is a myth in dance training that you have to start young – in fact learning can happen at any time, it just takes time.

The motivation to keep going is essential, and support, encouragement and access to qual-ity learning experiences motivate the endeavour to continue. The length and depth of that learning process means dancers have to work safely and with attention to their health and well-being, alongside a commitment to physical work and mental focus. Understanding what you are trying to achieve in your technical practice can support a positive and healthy learning process.

CHAPTER 2

THE ESSENTIALS OF GOOD TECHNIQUE

Class is for the dancer to get to know them-selves and how they work.[2]

EMBODIMENT

There are some fundamentals that underlie dance as a practice, and these are how we, as humans, are structured and function. A major feature of all dance practice is the fact that we have a particular structure to our body:

- Our eyes are at the front
- We have verticality, as we walk upright on two feet
- We have two symmetrical sides
- We have dexterous arms and hands that allow us to manipulate our environment
- We have skeletal, muscular, organ, fluid and fascial systems and functions that give us our shape and movement potentials
- We have bodily processes such as respiration, circulation and digestion
- We have senses that bring us information about the external environment – our *exteroceptors*
- We have senses that allow us to sense ourselves from the inside, through internal perception, so we feel our basic emotions such as hunger, we feel our relationship to gravity, and feel ourselves moving by sensing the positioning of our bones and the tones within our musculature. These are our *interioceptors*
- We have energy to use, but we also require recu-peration
- We exist in gravity
- We always need to support our weight in gravity
- If we let go, we move downwards
- To go up and counteract gravity we need force. We can use force to jump, but then we will come down again

Because of these things, human movement works in particular ways. We have our bodily structure, our *anatomy*, and a *physiology*, which is how it func-tions, and we use a certain force to move in gravity (assessing this use of force is *biomechanics*). The combination of these things gives rise to certain constructions for human movement, which we all learn through experimenting with movement as we grow as children, so we learn through experiencing with our integrated mind and body.

Dance learning works in the same way: we learn through doing, through experience and practice, enhanced and supported by a questioning and seeking outlook. By seeking to learn what we do and how we go about it, can change us. We can change and expand our understanding and our physical capabilities. Our learning is *embodied*, in that once we gain understanding/experience of something it makes us different; our body can change, our mental pathways and connections can change, and our interactions with our envi-ronment can change.

Bodily movement is normal: we are all built to move, but due to that normality the process of movement is forgotten and becomes merely an unconscious background to our lives. Dancers reawaken the conscious awareness of their movement capabilities, and they develop their expertise in dance through using the learning capabilities and possibilities that exist in and through ourselves as embodied people. This learning process involves the whole person in an

Fig. 10: Cunningham class taught by Hannah Cameron, featuring dancers Lewis Sharp, Aisha Stanley, Jessica Chambers and Holly Smith; Trinity Laban Conservatoire of Music and Dance, London. JAMES KEATES

WE ARE WHAT WE DO

Research is just starting to discover how our activities in life can create adjustments in the switching on and off of our genes. Rock climbers develop stronger finger bones because of the frequent demand for finger strength in what they do. Mountain rescuers can develop the capacity to take more oxygen out of thin air at altitude.

integration of mind and body, through doing, sensing, feeling, reacting, responding, reflecting, and so on. We also function as social beings who communicate with each other, and our social interactions are also structured. How we interact with others is a form of communication: we understand people by observing their movements, as much as anything else, and we ourselves are observed by others.

As dance is not just a physical exercise, but a social and communicative expressive form, becoming aware of ourselves as embodied beings within our social environment is a big step in gaining dance technique. We learn to use ourselves as individual people, as the medium for our practice requires a self-knowledge that infuses the learning process as much as our individual performance. We learn in group contexts, and we learn through collaboration, observation and interaction as much as through practice and direction.

Fig. 11: Partnering in motion: the head-tail connection. Release class taught by
Melanie Clarke, featuring dancers Alessandra Ruggeri and Luca Braccia; Trinity
Laban Conservatoire of Music and Dance, London. JAMES KEATES

Fig. 12: Class practice. Technique class taught by Hannah Cameron, featuring dancers Jessica Chambers and Alisha Stanley; Trinity Laban Conservatoire of Music and Dance, London. JAMES KEATES

The main aim of technique is to learn how to integrate movement intention with execution, so we can do what we decide we want to do. This involves understanding movement and how to achieve it, which involves an integration of the awareness of the sensation of motion with the result of motion, but also an understanding of how the result of that motion will be seen by others.

In order that you can become a creative dancer you need to gain knowledge of yourself and of the medium of dance. Understanding the constructions of dance as constructions from the patterns and structures of human movement can enable under-standing and choice-making in performance. These structures may be shared, but simultaneously every-body is different. Relating the ideas and structures to the reality of your bodily experience allows you to assimilate information within the internal sensorial experience of moving.

This approach means that you do not have to memorize factual information as a mental exercise, rather you experience and hold the knowledge in how you perceive your body moving as an inte-grated mind and body. You hold your knowledge in the substance of yourself as an embodied person. This method creates embodied knowing, and as such, is the medium and the result of learning to dance. Dance classes can facilitate generating this experiential knowing, and different techniques do this in different ways. Whatever the approach there can be many layers of information to take in.

THE STRUCTURE OF HUMAN MOVEMENT

Dance technique should enable the development of skill in controlled and aware use of energy to embody the content of the movement performed. All human movement shares five properties:

• Body
• Space
• Action
• Dynamics
• Relationships

Movements are a particular selection or emphasis of possibilities within these different components. All of these five properties are present in every movement. There has to be a body, and that body's actions in time and space create changes in the

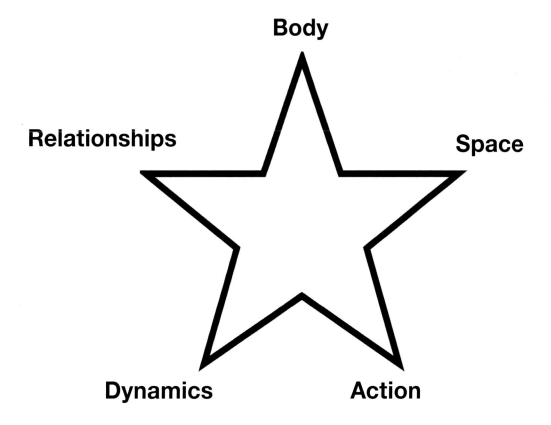

Fig. 13: Star diagram.

relationships between different parts of the body and between the body and its environment.

This model of the five constituents of movement is called the Structural Model of Human Movement. It came from the star diagram of the five properties of movement published by Valerie Preston-Dunlop,[3] a student and colleague of the choreographer and dance innovator, Rudolf Laban. The choreological practice teacher Rosemary Brandt then developed this model as a method for observation and embodiment of movement. By looking at movement through the lens of this structural model we can both observe and make choices about movement through understanding the possibilities within each of the five constituents of movement, and how those choices then inter-relate to create forms and structures in dance.

Different dance forms and different technical practices emphasize different possibilities within these five structures, and through that, different dance is created. Each contemporary dance technique discussed in this book is a particular set of choices in each of these five constituents. Understanding techniques through this lens will enable an understanding of the principles of the techniques and the distinctions between them, and will reveal how they are made. Understanding the principles can really help in understanding how to approach learning and performing these styles of movement, as well as the skills and abilities you can take from them.

BODY

'Body' involves the parts of the body: the limbs, the joints, the surfaces, the tissues, fluids and organs. We can bring attention to one aspect or part of the body, led from somewhere specific, or isolate a particular part. If we focus our movement from our joints, we can create foldings and unfoldings, angles and articulations. If we focus moving from our surfaces, we can create sweeping journeys through the air, whole body integrated curves or lines, fluid successions. We can move from our connectivity, our fluid structures, our organs, and what we are thinking about alters how we perceive ourselves. In the use of the body, where we place our attention will change how we move and the visual quality of our actions.

SPACE

We understand the space we inhabit through our body. We have a front, our eyes are orientated to that front, and our hips propel us in that direction, so we have the forward direction. We have a back and two symmetrical sides, so we have backward and sideways directions: this divides us with our sagittal (forwards/backwards) and lateral (right/left) dimensions. We sense the length of our spine and the passage of our digestive system, and thus feel the length of the torso with a sense of direction from the mouth to the anus. As we stand upright on two feet, we have a verticality, and thus we perceive the head as up and the feet as down, providing us with our vertical (up/down) dimension. Also, we sense the pull of gravity into the earth so we can have an up and a down based on the line of gravity even if we are not standing vertically.

We sense our other internal organs, and we sense the distance of these to the ends of our limbs, so we have a centre and peripheries. We have length to our limbs, which allows us to reach out from this centre, and through which we can interact and manipulate our environment.

These sensorial aspects of ourselves therefore bring meaning to the space immediately around us. We have space that we can reach with our body, which is like a three-dimensional field around us that we carry with us, which is known as the kinesphere. Within this kinesphere we can move between the dimensions, creating planes of motion:

- connecting the vertical and lateral dimension gives us the vertical or *door* plane (like standing within a door frame)
- connecting the vertical and sagittal dimensions gives us the sagittal or *wheel* plane (imagine a wheel rolling forwards or backwards)
- connecting the sagittal and lateral dimensions gives us the horizontal or *table* plane (horizontal to the floor, like a table top)

Our kinesphere then exists in general space, which is the space beyond our immediate reach. To orientate ourselves in dance practice we supply general space with meaning by extending the directions we understand from our body to provide perspectives, such as denoting a front, a back, a right and a left to the space. In technique classes often the front is denoted by where the teacher stands, as we need to see the teacher, and our eyes are orientated to the front because of where they are placed in our head. Sometimes a mirror might be the designated front in a studio space, but in a different class the mirror may be avoided to promote awareness of the sensation of moving, rather than external image.

Moving in space provides us with the possibility of having spatial intent, in how the commitment of energy from the body is used in space, and through which we can give space shape. Spatial intent can be a virtual phenomenon in that it is not real, but is an imagined intention, the effect of which can be communicated to an onlooker as an aspect of movement. Valerie Preston-Dunlop[4] delineates these virtual spatial forms in discrete categories, as discussed below.

Spatial Progression

Spatial progression is the name given to the idea of creating pathways in space. These pathways can be straight or curved. We can create these by travelling when our locomotion allows the pathway of our journey to be 'readable' to an observer, or we can do this within our kinesphere by drawing pathways in space with parts of the body. By moving we can create a sense of lines or curves in space – these pathways can sometimes be called *trace forms*. These pathways through space are virtual, as we are not actually creating a drawn line or a circle, but through our performance we allow something virtual to be perceived.

Spatial Projection

Spatial projection is the creation of another form of virtual line or curve in space, but this time it is not one left behind after our movement through space, but one that extends from the body out of the kinesphere. We project energy beyond the body so the directional properties of our body seem to reach beyond the end of our limbs or the limits of our tissues. We can project through our eyes in the act of looking, we can project beyond our limbs in the act of reaching. This virtual extension beyond the body requires a commitment of energy to movement, and can allow movement to seem bigger in space than the body itself.

Spatial Tension

In spatial tension the space between things becomes a perceivable aspect of our movement. A relationship across space is created, which generates a perceivable energy between things. An example of this is to hold an imaginary ball between your hands. The shaping in the hands creates a spherical shaping to the space between them. This imaginary sphere can grow and shrink and be rolled around in the hands, or even thrown about – however, it is completely virtual and not really there. Spatial tension can also be between two people, or between a person and an object, when there is a clear relationship set up and the space between becomes important.

Body Design

Body design is about the shaping created by the body itself, lines and curves in the body, rather than something created in the empty space around the body. However, this spatial embodiment can also be considered virtual, as the shape and positioning of the body creates visible lines and curves despite the actual anatomical structure of the body that performs them. If we aim to create a line in space with our arm, we utilize the longitudinal form of our arm to do that – but sticking an arm out into space is not enough, as the arm is not a line. If we consider the arm as a structure, we see it is curved and that the width changes. So when we create a line in space with our arm, we are creating a virtual phenomenon.

The same is true of a curve: our arm is made of bones and joints, and when we bend our joints we create angles between the bones, we do not create an actual curve – and yet we can make a curve perceivable by controlling the degree and relationships of the angles, and the placement of the hands in relation to those. So the perceivable form of the body in space is as much based on the focus and quality of our performance as spatial progression, spatial projection and spatial tension.

ACTION

Action refers to what the body does – the movement produced by the activity of the body in time and space. This can be referred to as the *form* of the movement. Action can be subdivided into categories, such as:

- Jumping – elevation of the body through a push off the ground, time in the air, and a landing
- Turning – revolving around the vertical axis of the body, which produces a change in orientation
- Travelling – moving the whole body through space towards or away from a location
- Transferring weight – shifting the support of the weight of the body, on the floor or another surface, from one part/area of the body to another
- Twisting – creating a torsion in the body around an axis, where one end of the body section turns more than the other
- Gesturing – moving a body part without affecting the rest of the body/ isolation of a body part
- Leaning – shifting the bodyweight off the vertical but only to the limit of recovery so you can bring yourself back to balanced verticality
- Falling – shifting the bodyweight and allowing it to lead you off balance, causing motion in space
- Closing – moving inwards towards the centre, getting smaller
- Opening – moving away from the centre, getting bigger
- Stillness – actively holding the body still so there is no movement

These action categories help us to distinguish movement intention and purpose, and yet are not specific to any particular style or technique of movement.

DYNAMICS

Dynamics refers to the quality of movement that stems from a particular approach to the use of energy. Energy is necessary to create any action in the body, but that energy can be manifested and directed differently to produce different qualitative emphasis and effect. Rudolf Laban divided the qualitative possibilities of movement into four *'motion factors': flow, force, time* and *space*, and he wrote about having an attitude towards movement that emerges as different combinations within and across these different motion factors.[5]

- Flow – is the spectrum of possibilities between *bound* and *free*. Free relates to the giving out of energy, and the lack of resistance to gravity, and a letting-go. Bound relates to an inward direction of energy, an energy not released into space but held within the skin: there is more resistance to gravity. Rudolf Laban related flow to emotion
- Force – (sometimes termed *Weight*) is a spectrum of possibilities between *strong* and *light*. Force relates to how we use our physical energy, the weight and power of our body. Rudolf Laban related *Force* to sensation
- Time – is a spectrum of possibilities between *sudden* and *sustained* and relates to speed of movement. Rudolf Laban related *Time* to intuition
- Space – is the spectrum of possibilities between *direct* and *indirect*, and relates to our attitude to how we use space. *Direct* relates to working in straight lines towards a destination, and penetrates space. *Indirect* (also sometimes called 'flexible') is when we work in curves that move around things, where we accommodate space and are adaptable. Rudolf Laban related *Space* to thinking

RELATIONSHIPS

Relationships refer to how one aspect of movement relates to the others. This could be within the structural model – how the action relates to the space and the dynamics. It can also work within part of the structural model – how different parts of the body relate to each other, or different aspects of space

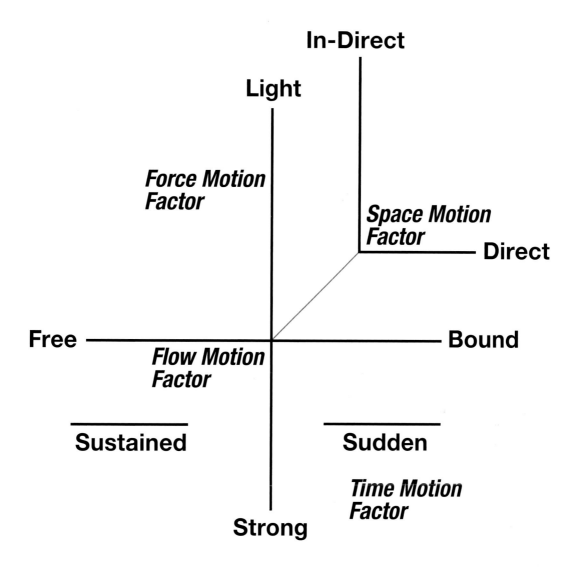

Fig. 14: Laban's effort graph.

relate to each other. Relationships are also about how the movement relates within its environment, whether that is the group participatory setting of a dance technique class, or in relation to the audience in a performance environment. (For more information refer to Preston-Dunlop (1998; 1980/2013).)

Particular aspects of the structures of human movement are used and emphasized in different dance forms, and dance techniques are particular constructions within these possibilities. A dance technique class provides the opportunity to experi-

ence a particular set of constructions and emphasis, and different technique classes provide opportunity to experience different sets of choices. Despite these differences between dance techniques there are some fundamental constructions that all share.

OVERLEAF: **Fig. 15: Learning in a group situation. Technique class taught by Hannah Cameron, featuring dancers Lewis Sharp, Aisha Stanley, Jessica Chambers and Holly Smith; Trinity Laban Conservatoire of Music and Dance, London.** JAMES KEATES

TECHNIQUE CLASSES

Dance technique classes will have a structure that supports the bodily process including an effective warm up to lengthen the muscles and fascia, mobilise the joints and raise the heart rate; an energetic flow to the overall structure so that the body does not cool but stays warm and ready to move; a chance to use information given or to explore ideas; the possibility of moving fully with the body through space; a chance to explore the idea of performance; and then a cool-down. The structure of classes enables a learning journey in a way that is healthy and supportive for the bodily process.

To allow dance to flow easily through you as you create it, with and through yourself, you need to work with the structures of the class and your bodily structures and functions. This comes down to having the right attitude to learning, being open and receptive to experiences and possibilities, whatever they might be. Although you may have preferences of approach, you need to see every opportunity to move as a way of building your experiential knowledge and thus your options and choices for movement expression. Technique teacher and dance pedagogy researcher Jamieson Dryburgh says that he wants his students 'to be in control; I want them to take risks, and I want them to grab hold of the opportunity of leaning'.[6]

Cunningham Technique teacher, Rachel Burn, agrees that students need to cultivate:

> ...a contentment with the process of learning and the process of investigating all the time, rather than maybe the sense that you have got it or you haven't got it...[an] attitude of exploration and learning, and that is how we operate as dancers always.[7]

Thus technique classes are a place of researching as much as doing. You are exploring how to enable movement execution through yourself as a medium, and to do that you have to have clarity of intention. That clarity can only come through exploring what you are trying to do, not only as a physical structure of the body, but also as a purpose. As teacher Tina Krasevec says, you need both 'curiosity and body knowledge'.[8] Dance class can be a place to constantly re-establish efficient and effective technical patterning, or a place for repeating poor habits. It can be easy to approach movement that you think you recognize in the same way every time – however, often you need to approach a movement differently, from a different perspective and with an open mind, in order to gain new knowledge and new experiences.

Moving should feel good even if it is challenging. Learning to inhabit your structures – your bones, joints, skin, musculature, your weight in gravity – and understand the relationships between these and the movement in time and space that you are making happen, can support clarity and ease of articulation. Sometimes it can feel that to work hard you have to use a lot of muscular effort and fight your

PATTERNS OF MOVEMENT RESPONSES IN US

Foster says: 'People pattern themselves with each new task. Every new chore we do, every new tool we use, and every new situation we are in, requires some kind of patterning process. Since the body is a dynamic, living system that never stays the same, the patterns of movement and posture either improve or digress; there is no status quo. Poor posture and faulty movement will worsen unless attended to. Thus, we either figure out the best way to use our bodies, or we fall back into habitual ways of doing things and rely on faulty habits.'[9]

Fig. 16: Dialogue and interaction in a technique class. Release class taught by Melanie Clarke, featuring dancer Holly Smith; Trinity Laban Conservatoire of Music and Dance, London. JAMES KEATES

WORKING FROM THE INSIDE

Burns says: 'You work in what your body does; you obviously push the limits of it, but you respect your body and know what your body is. There is nothing external that is governing that.'[10]

body; however, this is not the most productive and sustainable method of working. Staying relaxed and positive can support the maximizing of the range of motion you already possess. If you work from yourself, rather than from an idea of what you think you should be, then you can expand your possibilities and potentialities from the inside out.

ALIGNMENT

Clarity of body alignment, which essentially means the relationships and integration of the body, can support efficient movement as well as minimizing the potential risk of injury. Discovering how to feel these functional relationships can be the longest and most involved aspect of dance training; rather than something you get right before you move, it is something you work on, and with, continuously. Working with your

Fig. 17: Enjoying class practice. Release class taught by Melanie Clarke, featuring dancers Luca Braccia, Holly Smith and Rebecca Hunt; Trinity Laban Conservatoire of Music and Dance, London. JAMES KEATES

body and your relationship to gravity can enable a useful and functional alignment.

Our bodies are designed to move, but often the stresses of life and training, bad habits and fatigue result in habitual tension patterns that can disrupt the organization of the body. Habitual tension, or habitual movement practices that overload particular muscle groups, can become normalized and therefore no longer perceptually noticed. However, the result can often pull our alignment away from the simple efficiency that is designed into our structure.

A shift in the body alignment can then result in compensation patterns that add more tensions, which again can disrupt efficient movement, both through the energy lost in maintaining the tension, and the lesser capacity of tense muscles to contract and extend, leading to restriction to joint mobility. When there is good alignment, the structures of the body are in balance, and joint mobility and muscular power can be optimized.

ACTIVATING MOVEMENT

Berkeley-White says: 'In dance technique we are building skills, you are becoming increasingly conscious of what's already there, and through that consciousness activating it to a degree that you can use it for something. Gravity is always there, but if you can really use it, if you know how it works through you, you can use it to your advantage.'[11]

We want to maximize our efficiency, which means that we do not want to waste energy. The definition of efficiency is that we use our energy effectively to achieve our movement output. This is not about being lazy or not working, but rather about working in an optimal way so that we can use our energy well for the movement we want to do. Part of that is about moving with maximum ease and without strain, and spreading the effort of movement through the entire integrated body. Overexertion of one body area leads to fatigue, which means you have to stop. Working efficiently means you can maintain working for longer without exhaustion.

Effective and functional use of the body is part of working efficiently. A working muscle needs to contract and extend, but it is the movement

Fig. 18: Feeling the vertebrae. Release class taught by Melanie Clarke, featuring dancers Lewis Sharp, Alessandra Ruggeri and Luca Braccia; Trinity Laban Conservatoire of Music and Dance, London. JAMES KEATES

between contraction and extension that allows that muscle to be effective. Holding tension in muscles as a habit means the muscle cannot extend fully or contract fully, making it less effective in supporting movement. Holding tension also takes energy that is unnecessary and does not support the movement we want to do. So being strong as a dancer is not about having bulky muscles. Muscles are only strong and powerful when able to flow from full contraction to full release; a muscle that is constantly contracted even slightly will have no power to contract fully or to release fully, making it weak.[12]

Understanding the relationships in our body that enable good alignment is about discovering a balance of forces and movement of weight and energy. It is not about holding something in place, because that would inhibit moving. These relationships have to be understood through moving to support balance of the body in different situations. Thus, alignment has to be understood not just theoretically and not just when standing still, but in and through moving: so alignment has to be dynamic, which means living, breathing and dealing with changing situations.

Alignment of the anatomical structures should be viewed as a whole system, and never thought of in isolated parts. Correcting the alignment of one body part without viewing the body in relationship as an integrated whole will lead to tension and compensation, and thus new holding patterns, which can limit rather than support moving.

BREATHING

Good alignment is dynamic, and is always in flux due to the constant flow of motion through the internal structures of the body. Every 'in' breath is enabled through the ribcage lifting and opening and the diaphragm contracting, which expands the lungs and creates negative air pressure, drawing air in. Every 'out' breath is generated by the diaphragm releasing and the ribcage dropping, pushing air out of the lungs.

The constant wave of motion of the diaphragm from breathing creates motion through the lower torso in the lower organs, abdominal muscles and

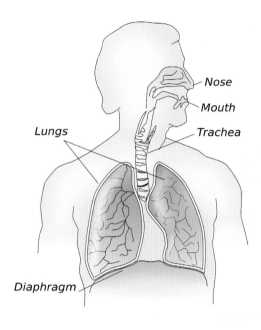

Fig. 19: The anatomy of breathing. PIXABAY

pelvic floor muscles. This flux in the lower body massages the organs, promoting fluid exchange in the cells of the body and helping oxygen to reach the cells. Depth of breathing is essential for a good oxygen supply to the body, to provide energy but also to promote calmness. Shallow breathing can create anxiety and promote tension through the association with the fight or flight response, whereas deeply breathing creates ease in the organs, which the brain responds to. A calm person has greater ability to focus their attention conducive to effective learning. Thus dynamic alignment is not possible without ease and depth of breathing.

This is why alignment cannot be something that is held: holding the ribcage down, holding the tummy in or holding the shoulders down will all restrict the motion of the body needed for ease of breath, creating anxiety and restriction as well as motion-reducing tension. Ease in the torso for effective breathing patterns is often thought to be contradictory to ideas of strength, as popular theories concerning the engagement of energy and commitment to physical training promote the idea that muscles have to be constantly contracted.

Fig. 20: Feeling the breath: Graham class taught by Geneviève Grady, featuring dancers Natalya Smith, Kirbie Franks and Anna Broome; Trinity Laban Conservatoire of Music and Dance, London. JAMES KEATES

CENTRE

BODY CENTRE

The word 'strength' is also often used in relation to the 'core' or the 'centre' (a word often used in all forms of movement training, but frequently misunderstood). The word 'centre' can be used to indicate many different things, and its meaning can change from one technique to another. There is a 'body centre', which is the central point in the length, width and depth of the torso, somewhere behind the belly button – in fact this centre is sometimes called 'navel centre'. If you place yourself in a big X shape, and imagine lines through the body from the right hand to the left foot, the right foot to the left hand, and from the top of the head to the tail, these lines would intersect at this body centre.

As the navel was where the umbilical cord connected to us as a developing foetus in the womb, this centre can be seen as a specific point of nourishment, interconnection and development, which is referred to as 'core-distal connectivity' by Peggy Hackney.[13] 'Navel radiation' is a concept related to this centre, where the peripheries (the ends of limbs and the edges of the body) have a relationship to the navel centre: thus closing actions bring the peripheries in towards the centre, and opening actions spread the peripheries away from this centre. It could be thought of as a constellation, in which relationships between body parts can be seen in relation to this central connecting point.

BODY-PART CENTRES

Each body segment can also be said to have a centre. Every joint can be seen as a centre for part of a limb, the point from which movement happens. So the elbow can be a centre for movement of the lower arm, the hip joint a centre for movement of the leg. This creates a theoretical sphere of potential motion, or kinesphere, for each body segment. This many-centred approach is used in the symbol

Fig. 21: Internal sensing of the back of the skull. Release class taught by Melanie Clarke, featuring dancers Alessandra Ruggeri and Luca Braccia; Trinity Laban Conservatoire of Music and Dance, London. JAMES KEATES

system for recording movement – 'Labanotation' (also known as 'Kinetography Laban'), which was instigated by the dance pioneer Rudolf Laban and then developed by his followers, including Albrecht Knust and Ann Hutchinson-Guest.

This system is used for recording dances as well as for the analysis of movement of all forms[14] to allow for specific analysis of placement and movement for all parts of the body. Awareness of the movement in our joints arises from sensory receptors located in the skin and connective tissues called propriocep-tors. Proprioceptors in joint capsules and ligaments provide perception of joint position and movement.[15] A sense of the positioning of the bones in space also comes from the eyes, in seeing the changes in the body happening, or from the ears, in feeling changes in gravity for the head.

LOWER AND UPPER CENTRE

There is also a lower centre and an upper centre. The lower centre, or centre of gravity, is contained in the lower belly (that is, lower than the navel centre). When standing upright it is situated in the pelvis just in front of the upper part of the sacrum at about 54–55 per cent of the height of the individual if measuring up from the floor, and midway between the front and back of the body.[16] This centre is important for balance, as it must be above the point of support on the floor, or within the area of support on the floor, in the line of gravity, so the body does not fall when in an upright position. Thus the centre of gravity needs to be over the foot when balancing on one leg.

If you find this balance and then start to shift the centre of gravity, you will feel gravity starting to pull you off balance. We can perform this shift of the lower centre and not fall by counterbalancing the supporting part with other parts of the body such as the head, or by holding on to something, such as a partner or a ballet barre. So when in motion, and particularly when the torso is in motion, the centre of gravity can change, and actually at times

Fig. 22: Sensing the skull leading the spine. Release class taught by Melanie Clarke, featuring dancers Yu-Tzu Lin and Lewis Sharp; Trinity Laban Conservatoire of Music and Dance, London. JAMES KEATES

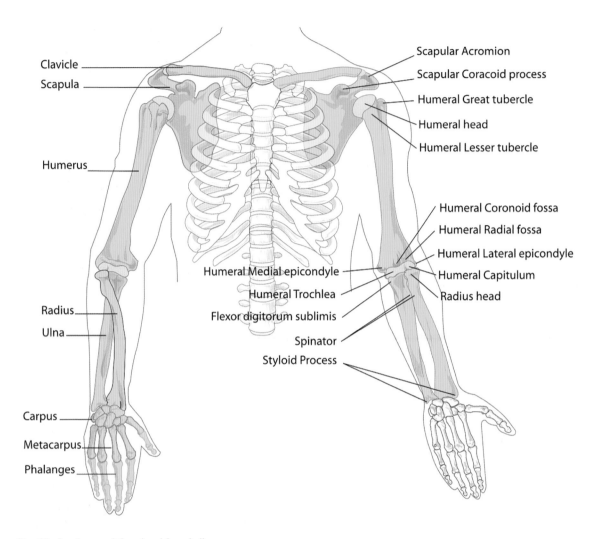

Fig. 23: Anatomy of the shoulder girdle. PIXABAY

be outside the body.[17] As the torso constitutes about 50 per cent of our bodyweight, when we move it our weight shifts, and then our point of balance can be between counterbalancing points such as the head and pelvis. 'Movements that involve continuous change in the orientation of the body segments to each other result in continuous change in the body's centre of gravity'.[18]

The upper centre, or centre of expressiveness, is in the chest behind the breast bone, near the heart. This is the centre for the constellation of movement in the upper limbs, including the upper spine and head. Moving the arms in relation to the upper centre creates inter-relationships and support for arm

actions in space from the entire shoulder girdle and upper torso. The bony connections from the hands to the shoulder joint continue both through the collar bones (clavicles – see Figure 23) to the breast bone (sternum) and through the shoulder blades (scapular); connective tissues also establish relationships between the bony structures in different lines so the hands inter-relate with the breast bone, shoulder blades, shoulder joints and the spine. Working with these connections allows for an integrated support structure as well as greater expressive possibilities. It can also increase the spatial range and reach of the upper body simply by being a more complex set of movement possibilities within literally a longer chain.

ABDOMINALS

Centre is sometimes used to refer to the abdominal muscles, or is orientated to a particular layer of these. The rectus abdominal (commonly known as the 'six-pack') is the best known of the abdominal muscles, but often dance teachers want students to work with the lower layer of abdominal muscles – the transversus abdominis – that surrounds the lower torso and is connected with the act of breathing. Any of these centres can become a point of holding – something fixed and immobile, which can inhibit free-flowing movement and access to depth of experience. Working from one of these centres is to work with it as a place of connection and relationship, and not as something fixed and anchored.

THE CORE

There is another concept of centre that is not a point or an area of the body, but rather a long connection from feet to head. This centre is known as the 'core', and an apple core is the image that is often used to support an understanding of it. It is a structure of the deepest layer of the body, which is aligned to our vertical length. This structure is made of continuous connective tissue. The fascial tissues create layers of support around other tissues in the body, such as the bags that contain muscle tissues and connect muscle tissues to bones, and the fascial bags that surround organs. However, these fascial tissues are not separate, but form continuous chains through the body. This core is explained beautifully in the book *Anatomy Trains* by Thomas Myers (2014) under the sub-title 'Deep Front Line'.

The image of an apple core is useful as it is a vertical structure that has three-dimensional form and connects the top of the apple to the bottom, and is the centre of all the other tissue that surrounds it – and as the apple core contains the pips, the core connectivity contains the organs of the body. The core, or deep front line, starts at one end inside the arches of the feet, and continues in the deepest layer of muscle behind the shin bones. The fascia continues around the inner thigh muscles into the pelvic floor, and becomes the bags of tissue that contain the organs as well as the iliopsoas. These

Fig. 24: Partnering in improvization. Release class taught by Melanie Clarke, featuring Melanie Clarke and dancer Luca Braccia; Trinity Laban Conservatoire of Music and Dance, London. JAMES KEATES

continue into the diaphragm itself, and then the bags of tissue that contain the heart and lungs, travelling up the front of the cervical spine to end where the jaw hinges on to the skull.[19]

The key to core activation is, then, integration in and to the deepest tissue layers of the body. Integration is supported by balance of the other fascia chains in the body. Thus this centre is not muscle tissue at all, but a long chain of connective tissue that can contain muscles and organs within it, as well as acting as a carrier for proprioceptive receptors – the nerve endings that provide sensorial information to our brain about the state of our body.

CONNECTIVITY

The fascia chains through the body produce interconnection and integration, therefore each muscle is part of an integrated system that works in relationship. Our alignment can be supported in ways that we do not perceive as needing effort. Moshe Feldenkrais provides an example of what he calls *anti-gravity* muscles as those that hold the eyelids open, which we do not have to control or think about.[20] The diaphragm and heart are muscles that work ceaselessly and never tire, and yet we do not actively control them. Thus we do not need to hold ourselves up with felt muscular effort: rather, we need to allow our body to work in gravity with integration and balance, so that dynamic alignment feels effortless.

STRENGTH

Franklin says: 'Powerful movement is created if the whole system of muscles, bones and other tissue works together in a coordinated way. The interplay of the parts of the whole structure, and not isolated muscle power, is crucial for effective strength.'[21]

Dynamic alignment is not about fixing a state and place to be, but about finding the appropriate place in your relationship to gravity to support the movement you are doing. Balancing body energy can be important, in that excess tension in parts of the body can disrupt that balance in gravity, as it affects the

Fig. 25: A tensegrity toy.

whole structure. Good alignment requires balancing our skeleton within our connectivity structures. The connective tissues, or fascia, are the strong fibres that create shape and support for the soft tissues of the body, and connect the bones of the skeleton together across the joints as ligaments and tendons. These connecting structures create webs and lines of interconnection through the body, and are the basis for our bodily integration.

Understanding connectivity requires us to think about our bodies as a balanced system of inter-relationships and not as a fixed structure. Our bodies are *tensegrity* structures. The word 'tensegrity' comes from a combination of the words 'tension' and 'integrity'. A tensegrity structure is one in which the integrity of the structure, its support and shaping, is based on the relationships of all the constructing elements. There are hard elements that act as spacers, and elastic elements that hold those spacers in a pattern through a web of forces.

In a tensegrity toy, if one element is moved or compressed, the impact of that is shared across the whole interconnected system, and the whole shape changes – and if the compression is released, the shape can spring back into balance. In the skeleton our bones act as spacers within the elastic web of our connective tissues. Our bones do not touch, but are supported to maintain relationships across joints. Movement of one part can influence the entire structure, and thus the whole body absorbs and reflects any change; then the body can also return to a state of balanced distribution of forces. Understanding the relationship of skeletal structures and the lines of connectivity can support clarity of movement and dynamic alignment, as the whole integrated body supports the changes, and absorbs the impact of motion, as well as enabling a re-balancing, which is a release rather than imposing strain.

The first process in pursuing a dynamic alignment is to start to notice where you might be holding tension and creating imbalance. Looking at yourself moving on video, or asking someone to look at your alignment, can be a way to inform yourself about tension patterns that you have become so used to

Fig. 26: Feedback from the teacher. Technique class taught by Hannah Cameron, featuring dancers Jessica Chambers and Alisha Stanley; Trinity Laban Conservatoire of Music and Dance, London. JAMES KEATES

that you cannot feel them any more. Noticing simple imbalances – such as one shoulder being higher than the other, the front of the chest being more open than the back, or more weight being placed through one supporting leg than the other – can start to reveal patterns of holding and inhibiting.

This external observation and feedback can be a useful detector, but should not become the means of correction. Shifting your alignment so that it looks right is not a productive solution. Rather, start to try and become aware of the tension through feeling it – that is, become aware of the sensation of the tension again. Check to see if you are aware of holding, and try to see if you can let go (somatic practices or movement therapy, including massage, can help with this). If you can start to undo a block through a process of awareness, rather than trying to hold yourself in what you think might look right, you will start to discover a dynamic, living, breathing, moving alignment. As Release-based Technique teacher David Waring says:

What I feel I notice in teaching is that often people's anchor is either in the pelvis and hip sockets and holding there, or in the shoulders and ribcage and holding there, in order to give them some sense of control and security. And of course, there is a lack of dynamic in the breath there because it is not going to be free in certain moments; and therefore, that block means that the body isn't moving with as much application as it could, or moving in a way whereby the consequence of one thing is very clearly read through the rest of the body.[22]

GROUNDEDNESS

Dynamic alignment is also associated with groundedness, which refers to the relationship to the floor and gravity. Peggy Hackney describes this as follows:

In everyday language, to say that someone is 'grounded' implies that that person has a stable sense of him/herself. This presence of self requires an embodied relationship to the earth. Every cell which is in contact with the earth (oftentimes the soles of the feet) can experience connection by yielding weight into the earth and feeling matched by the earth's support. Movement can then travel through the body, utilizing that sense of grounded stability as a base from which to move. A simple question is often helpful, 'How am I connecting with the earth?'[23]

As contemporary dance technique is practised without shoes, the feet can actually feel the floor directly. So becoming aware of, and experimenting with, the contact between the soles of the feet and the floor can be really important as part of dynamic alignment. Contemporary techniques

Fig. 27: Hanging over. Technique class featuring dancers Anna Broome and Alice Lovrinic; Trinity Laban Conservatoire of Music and Dance, London.
JAMES KEATES

use both parallel leg/feet positions and turned out feet/leg positions, where the rotation in the hips changes the positioning of the legs under the pelvis, and thus the placement of the feet on the floor. Gaining an embodied understanding of the relationships between the bones of the legs and feet, and how the weight is distributed above and below the ankle, can be an important technical achievement.

The toes also contribute to support and engagement with the floor through the foot (gripping toes can actually pull the balls of the feet off

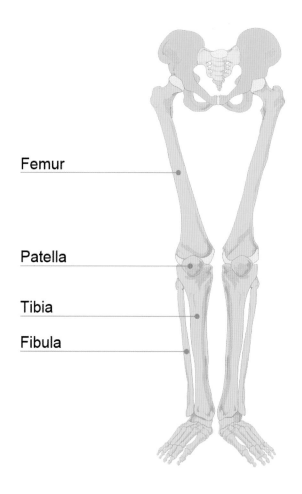

Femur

Patella

Tibia

Fibula

Fig. 28: Back view of the bones of the lower legs and feet. WIKIMEDIA COMMONS

the floor, which can really affect balance) – trying to relax the toes and feel all ten toes touching the floor can be important knowledge to gain. Shifting the distribution of weight around the feet can be a way of allowing sensation to inform you of the possibilities for this base of support in gravity. Groundedness when not standing can also be influenced by the sensation of touching the floor, so becoming aware of sensation can be an important technical consideration.

WEIGHT DISTRIBUTION IN THE FEET

Arches are very strong structures, where the weight is supported equally on both supports, which allow the arch to meet in the centre with perfectly balanced force. The strength created in this can then support a lot of weight above it without collapsing.

The arches of our feet work in the same way. For example, the distal end of the big toe metatarsal (the ball of the foot at the base of the big toe) is one support for the medial (inside) arch of the foot, and the calcaneus (heel bone) is the support for the other side. In struggling to find balance on one leg it is possible to actually take the inside edge of the ball of the foot (the distal end of the big toe metatarsal) off the floor, causing supination (inward flexion) of the ankle and thus lack of support through the medial arch and lack of clarity for the alignment of the leg and balance of the weight of the body above it. This can cause the task of supporting the weight of the body to be distributed more to the fibular – the thinner, more lateral shin bone – rather than using the strength of the tibia, which is the thicker and stronger of the shin bones, and relates with a bigger surface area to the talus of the ankle.

It can also cause greater force to be applied through the more lateral muscles in the thigh, taking the support away from the inner thigh muscles and the core connectivity. However, when seeking to find fluency of weight and use of weight to initiate motion in space, shifting the weight across the feet can allow the flow of weight through the body structures in a useful way, allowing you to achieve the motion you wish to find.

Thus, exploring and becoming aware of the weight distribution in the feet can support a truly dynamic alignment that is appropriate and applicable to the movement you wish to do.

Fig. 29: Hands-on work, exploring the structures and alignment of the leg. Release class taught by Melanie Clarke, featuring dancer Lewis Sharp; Trinity Laban Conservatoire of Music and Dance, London.

JAMES KEATES

DYNAMIC ALIGNMENT

Thus, accessing dynamic alignment can be about connecting to sensation and releasing inhibitors to balance and ease, and finding efficiency in motion in gravity. When working in an integrated and efficient way, movement aids the acquisition of strength, power, mobility, stability, clarity in space and ease. When we try and control alignment, especially by trying to make the body look right, we can inhibit breathing and not allow for the free movement of the body. Working on connecting your breath to the movement of the body can bring these vital aspects of alignment and ease into relationship.

Breath can be intentional and active in that you can focus on it as an aspect of what you are doing with your body, and this practice can be a useful exercise. Breath can also be something that you just notice already happening, and that noticing promotes awareness of breathing patterns.

You can try and listen to your breath, notice its rhythm, and the movement of the body in the act of breathing. You can use your hands to feel the motion of the breath in the torso, placing your hands in one place for a few breaths, and then moving them to feel the motion of the ribcage, the breast bone, the belly, the back.

Another useful way to sense your breath is in the bath with your ears under the water, as the water amplifies the sound and you can literally hear yourself breathe. See if you can then take that awareness into your life, including into technique class, and

Fig. 30: Concentration and focus. Graham class taught by Geneviève Grady, featuring dancers Jessy NacKay and Natalya Smith; Trinity Laban Conservatoire of Music and Dance, London. JAMES KEATES

see how it can enable you to be calm and release tension and find a greater feeling of effortlessness.

FOCUS AND ATTENTION

All these aspects of learning need focus and attention. One of the things you need to cultivate as a dancer is stamina of attention. Maintaining focus on your embodied experience takes a commitment that is different from, and simultaneous with, muscular effort. You can then commit your energy to the movement you are doing with a fullness that can fill your movement with intention. Developing this ability to stay focused in

practice is about quality of learning so you can get the most out of your experiences; this should develop alongside your strength, balance, mobility and precision.

What can support this focused attention is the feeling of safety in your dance practice, where you feel able to try things, explore things, and make mistakes at times. You also need enough recuperation time to recover your energy, and also to assimilate your experiences and the information you gain from them – so then you can make the most of the very focused time in class. If you can bring your whole self to your learning and be open to the experiences, you will learn effectively.

CHAPTER 3

GRAHAM TECHNIQUE

BACKGROUND AND PRINCIPLES

Martha Graham, an American dance artist and choreographer, created a form of dance technique as an expression of her choreographic vision, which became known as Graham Technique.

Martha Graham was born in 1894 in the USA. She was a powerful personality who forged a new form of theatre in the USA in the twentieth century. She started her dance experience at the age of nineteen in classes in expressive dance as part of a general art programme at the Comnock School of Expression, an experimental junior college in Los Angles, USA. Then in 1916, at the age of twenty-two, she joined the Denishawn School of Dancing and Related Arts, founded and run by Ruth St Denis and Ted Shawn in Los Angeles. She then joined the Denishawn dance company; after seven years with them she left to start exploring her own choreography. She presented her first independent work in New York City in 1926.

She founded the Martha Graham Studio in 1927 in New York City, where the Martha Graham School of Contemporary Dance continues today. She danced in her own work until 1969, and then continued to direct and choreograph for her company. She created 181 works, and presented her final complete choreography in 1990. She died in 1991 at the age of ninety-seven.

In Denishawn, Graham explored a physical expression and use of the body that had many different influences. Ruth St Denis drew dance ideas from East Asian dance and East Asian movement practices to create new dance work that was exotic for American audiences. She taught yoga and other Eastern practices, or movements derived from them. Ted Shawn, Ruth St Denis' husband and partner in the company, developed a technique practice to train dancers that was strong and physical and incorporated different elements, including ballet.

So Graham's career evolved from a basis of movement experimentation, the development of new movement work influenced by a variety of dance and movement forms. As a choreographer, Martha Graham started to explore movement in her own body, seeking a new form of expression. She developed and performed solo works with a frequency and rapidity that propelled her movement investigations onwards as she sought her own form of theatre for the twentieth century.

As a solo artist Graham started to develop critical acclaim, which brought new audiences to her work, and dancers who wanted to learn from her. She started to teach dancers who were drawn to her, and developed an ensemble group. She was prolific, creating over sixty new dances between 1926 and 1930.[24] Many of her early solo works she abandoned, as she wasn't interested in preserving them (although some were captured on film); rather, she used them to develop her artistry. Her later works, however, have become well known, and are part of the Graham Company Repertoire.

She was known to be an inspiring and charismatic teacher who spoke from her own experience as a dancer and performer, as well as using the artistic, historic and poetic references she drew inspiration from as a choreographer. 'Her dancers often recall the evocative way she spoke to convey a step, or to give them the right image connected to that step.'[25]

The emotional resonance of movement was very important to Martha. She said: 'The function of the

Fig. 31: *Diversions of Angels* by Martha Graham, reconstructed with students at Trinity Laban Conservatoire of Music and Dance, 2010. TRINITY LABAN © KYLE STEVENSON

Fig. 32: *Primitive Mysteries* by Martha Graham, reconstructed with students at Trinity Laban Conservatoire of Music and Dance. TRINITY LABAN © KYLE STEVENSON

Fig. 33: Contraction on the knees. Graham class taught by Geneviève Grady, featuring dancers Kirbie Franks and Anna Broome; Trinity Laban Conservatoire of Music and Dance, London. JAMES KEATES

dance is communication',[26] and 'It comes from the depths of man's inner nature, the unconscious'.[27] This emotional resonance is an important aspect of the performance mode for the practice of Graham Technique. However, the body communicates with an emotional energy in a visceral way that comes from the centre of the body. The intention is that the bodily expression is honed 'so that it can express the intention of every movement through the clarity of the movement itself'.[28]

This physical expression was placed as the central aspect of her choreography. A dancer in the

Fig. 34: Pleadings. Graham class taught by Geneviève Grady, featuring dancers Mitchell Davis and Pagan Hunt. Trinity Laban Conservatoire of Music and Dance, London. JAMES KEATES

Graham Company, S. Maslow, stated that Graham's aim was 'to make the human body an instrument that would be capable of expressing all things in human experience, not just pretty things. Sometimes they were ugly things. The movement was strong, sometimes very angular'.[29]

The dynamics of her choreography were visceral, animalistic. Gone is the courtly expression, and the lightness and ethereal quality so predominant in the romantic ballet of the nineteenth century. Martha said: 'You're not going to dance in a ballroom; you're not in a court situation. We're not interested in courtly behavior, in ballrooms. This is ground, these are pebbles, these are rocks.'[30]

THE TECHNIQUE

Graham developed her technique over many years. She added to it as her career progressed, her knowledge grew, and her choreography changed and

Fig. 35: Geneviève Grady leading a class in travelling tilts. Graham class taught by Geneviève Grady, featuring dancers Alice Lovrinic, Anna Broome, Federica Bertani, Mitchell Davis, Pagan Hunt, Rosemary Copp, Kirbie Franks, Jeanne Delévaque and Laure Dubanet; Trinity Laban Conservatoire of Music and Dance, London. JAMES KEATES

explored new things. Agnes De Mille, the choreographer and lifelong friend of Martha Graham, states that 'as soon as any new technique was clarified, it was used in a dance – or rather, the technique and the dance evolved together in simultaneous creation.'[31] Graham's movement exploration concentrated on the torso. Agnes De Mille describes it thus:

Martha knew that all emotion is visible in the torso because of body chemistry and mechanics....Arch the spine and you have emotion.... The arms and the face are peripheral, like the hair. It is the torso – heart, lungs, stomach, viscera, and, above all, spine – which express.

In the technique she developed, most of this exploration of the torso was done sitting on the floor. However, there were many different forms of practice that developed into the technique as it is today. Dorothy Bird, a dancer in the company between

1931 and 1937, stated that they worked on big torso swings; Sophie Maslow, a dancer with the company from 1931 until 1944, states that what they did in the early years depended on the period: 'There were times when we never went into the air, and then there were times when she'd concentrate on jumps.'[32]

So there is a vast heritage to this technique because of the length of time of Graham's working practice – but there was also time for the technique to be honed into an identified approach. The technical practice became a codified practice with established exercises and names given to actions and combinations, and a particular ordering of exercises through the class. When Graham stopped dancing, others took over the main roles in her works and also started to carry the legacy of the technique within the company. Dancers disseminated the technique in schools and colleges in the US and then abroad; Robert Cohen CBE (dancer in the Graham company from 1946) was very important in bringing the practice to the UK when he took up the position of artistic director of London Contemporary Dance Theatre in 1966. Over time the main carriers of the form developed their own lineages through their students, who passed on the technique through their teaching.

With Graham's death in 1991 people started to wonder how to hold on to the heritage of her work. Martha Hill says in the book *Goddess: Martha Graham's Dancers Remember*: 'If Martha [Graham] had continued to work and had continued dancing, her technique would have been changing to the end. She was a constant mover – her ideas were active.'[33] Now, in the twenty-first century, practitioners are seeking ways to maintain a historic legacy, but also to apply the physical and performative experiences of the technical approach to twenty-first-century dancers and training programmes.

The Graham Company continues to perform signature Graham works as well as new commissions and interpretations from contemporary artists inspired by Graham's legacy. The Graham School (marthagraham.edu) continues to train dancers, some of whom go into the company. Current teachers of Graham Technique in dance institutions with a varied technical curriculum are exploring principles embedded in the technique, and enabling access to the physical logic and depth of the practice in different ways. In this way the practice is used as an approach to learning dance using a particular heritage, as well as an application of contemporary knowledges and teaching approaches. Trinity Laban teacher Geneviève Grady says:

> As a teacher...the question becomes, how can I work with the integrity of this gathered information that we call Graham Technique? What I am doing at a conservatoire is that I am negotiating the various individual needs of the students, and examining through the practice of class choreography how they can best be served by what the technique already contains.[34]

Sarah Sulemanji, Graham Technique teacher at Middlesex University, agrees:

> Even though it is a codified technique... I feel that there is licence there for development and personal expression and freedom with the vocabulary, and those core principles that underpin that... It is a template.[35]

THE BODY
CONTRACTION, RELEASE AND SPIRAL

The primary features and fundamental physical actions of the Graham Technique are contraction, release and spiral. Contraction and release are based on the patterns of breathing.

As we exhale the diaphragm lifts, the abdominals draw back, the pelvic floor muscles lift, the breast bone comes in, and the ribs come closer together. These automatic actions expel air from the body. As we inhale the opposite happens: the diaphragm goes down, the abdominals and pelvic floor muscles release, the breast bone lifts and the rib cage expands to draw air into the body. Martha Graham took this fundamental aspect of being alive as a human as the very basis of her movement investigation in dance. The contraction and release

Fig. 36: Feeling the breath. Graham class taught by Geneviève Grady, featuring dancers Mitchell Davis, Kirbie Franks, Alice Lovrinic and Anna Broome; Trinity Laban Conservatoire of Music and Dance, London. JAMES KEATES

THE MOVEMENT OF BREATHING

When you inhale:

- the diaphragm contracts and lowers
- the ribs lift and open away from each other
- the lungs expand three-dimensionally
- the breast bone lifts
- the fascia wraps more tightly around the joints in the spine, and the spine lengthens
- the belly expands
- the pelvic floor expands
- the lower organs move

When you exhale:

- the diaphragm releases and lifts
- the ribs drop and come closer together
- the lung volume reduces three-dimensionally
- the breast bone drops
- the fascia releases and the spine settles into its curves
- the belly wraps closer around the spine
- the pelvic floor muscles lift
- the lower organs move

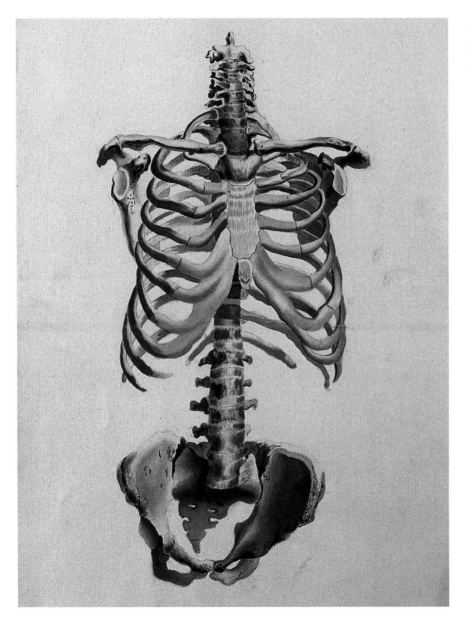

within the technique are very full expressions of the physical process of exhalation and inhalation, and utilizes and exemplifies this human act to create a theatrical dance form. Thus, the roots of the technical form are organic in nature, as it springs from the nature of the body itself and the subjective experience of moving.

The full embodiment of contraction and release creates a visceral action of drawing in and expanding out from the torso, making the action within the torso an instigator for the movement of the limbs and the movement of the body in space. Thus, these fundamentals are used across the whole technique, from sitting exercises to standing exercises, travelling and jumping.

Contraction
Contraction is a full expression of the motion involved in exhaling. The pelvic floor muscles contract, drawing the sitting bones towards each

Fig. 38: Contraction. Graham class taught by Geneviève Grady, featuring dancers Anna Broome, Pagan Hunt and Kirbie Franks; Trinity Laban Conservatoire of Music and Dance, London. JAMES KEATES

other and the tail in; the deep abdominal muscles contract, hollowing the belly; lengthening the spine and lifting the belly, as this deepens the pelvis and spine more to create a long curve in the torso. This action can be initiated consciously and purposefully from the pelvic floor and the abdominals, rather than being an increase in muscular effort at the end of an exhale; a contraction can also be done with an inhale providing a different experience for the dancer, so the breath is not prescribed but must be explored to

access the expressive potential of the action. This means that it becomes more abstracted, although not separated, from the act of breathing. Geneviève Grady says: 'Sometimes the breath will move first, and sometimes it is the tissues that move the breath.'[36] Breathing deeply can be a way to discover the sensation of the contraction, and breathings is the name of an exercise in the technique.

Gertrude Sturr, a member of Martha Graham's first ensemble group, is said to have explained that

Fig. 39: Sitting upright on the floor. Graham class taught by Geneviève Grady, featuring dancers Alice Lovrinic, Anna Broome and Mitchell Davis; Trinity Laban Conservatoire of Music and Dance, London. JAMES KEATES

they used vocalizing to support the experience of the contraction: 'For many years we were making the consonant "ssss". Martha [Graham] would say "sssss,sss" and let out the whole breath, then ask "What do the shoulders do? What do the hips do? What does the spine do?".' The contraction could also be done with a 'percussive force, like a cough',[37] which creates a sudden contraction of the diaphragm, expelling air from the lungs. The bodily activities of laughing and crying are manifested in the same physiological structures as breathing. Therefore exploring the physical sensations underlying laughing and crying can be used as ways for students of Graham Technique to first explore contraction.

Geneviève Grady describes the contraction as 'deeply inward', and arising from the deep lift of the pelvic floor.[38] Sara Sulemanji says:

Gather everything, lift everything from the inside, engage all of the pelvic floor muscles and transverse muscles so that those things are lifted but try to create space and opposition in that place as opposed to holding and gripping.[39]

This lifting within the movement is important, so that, even though there is a strong connection to the floor, the movement does not give in to the ground but resists it and springs off from it. As Frieda Flier, a dancer in the Graham company from 1936 to 1941, describes: 'You didn't fall on the floor, you bounced. You were resisting the floor.'[40] The pelvis is weighted, as it is the primary support of the body on the floor, but there is a feeling of an upward energy from the primary initiation in the base of the pelvis. The lumber spine lengthens into flexion as the pelvis tips posteriorly, and as the diaphragm lifts, energy travels upwards to the heart and chest. In some contractions this upward energy is fully expressed in a backward tilt of the head, so the face lifts. In other contractions, if the upward energy is felt internally but does not manifest itself in the action of the head, than the flexion of the spine becomes emphasized instead.

Release
Release is the movement that Graham established from the act of inhaling, which involves letting go of the contraction and lengthening the torso. Everything in the body extends between the top of the

Fig. 40: Fourth position spiral. Graham class taught by Geneviève Grady, featuring dancers Mitchell Davis, Anna Broome and Federica Bertani; Trinity Laban Conservatoire of Music and Dance, London. JAMES KEATES

head and the sitting bones to create a visual line. Inhaling during the release helps to support the lengthening of the torso through inflating the lungs and lengthening the spine. This lengthening can be into the vertical, or tilted forwards from the hip into a forward incline. The release involves moving the pelvis and releasing the patterning of the contraction. The sitting bones move apart a little, and the tail bone shifts back as the contraction of the pelvic floor muscles reduces, although the pelvic floor does not fully release.[41] The action of the release can draw air into the lungs, so inhaling can happen as a result and as an instigator.

Spiral
Spiral involves twisting the torso. The torso is extended long, and the twist is initiated from the torso rather than from the limbs or the head. When sitting, the spiral can be initiated from the sitting bones by shifting one sit-bone back; when standing, the spiral is more likely to be initiated higher in the torso than in the sit-bones, to maintain the alignment of the legs and not cause twisting in the knees.

The spiral utilizes a lengthening in the fascial connectivity known as the *functional lines*[42] or *cross lateral lines*[43], which connects one shoulder (and upper arm) across the torso to the opposite hip (and upper leg). This connectivity relates upper/lower body movement as well as left/right body movement. It also relates the oppositional limbs to the torso (as in the oppositional swing of the arm in walking).

These lines of connectivity are duplicated in front of the spine and ribs and behind the spine and ribs, creating two layers. If you spiral by drawing back the right shoulder blade you will open the front, cross-lateral, upper right to lower left connection. There can also be a sense of a drawing inwards from the right shoulder blade (scapula) towards the opposite hip across the back of the body. You will also, simultaneously, draw the left shoulder forwards away from the right leg, and lengthen the back upper left to lower right cross-lateral connection.

The cross-lateral connectivity/functional lines are most readily accessible through normal walking, because in this action the swing of the arm opposes the swing of the leg, creating a natural opposition. To do this there is a small rotational flow through the torso. To find the spiral, Sarah Sulemanji starts with walking both on the feet and the sitting bones:

How would you be if you are walking? How would you be if you were walking and you didn't spiral? You could work with the two halves of the body – what does that do to your body? Then, when you walk normally, what are you doing, where is that initiation from, and how?[44]

So the spiral is not an act of maximizing the rotation of the spine, but a feeling of opposition in the down/up, right/left, upper torso/lower torso polarities. Agnes De Mille says that Graham described the spiral thus: '...one has to work around one's own spine. One makes a spiral around the back. The flesh and body are wrapped around the bones.'[45]

In Graham spirals the head sometimes does not follow the twist, and the cervical spine actually rotates in the opposite direction, so the head direction is over the forward shoulder. This means there is another oppositional energy in the direction of the front of the shoulders and of the face. Geneviève Grady states that she often talks about '...the back shoulder blade...it is becoming what feels like my standing side, and the front shoulder blade feels like it is expressing into the space.'[46] Sarah Sulemanji describes images she was taught and that she uses in her teaching, which help with spiral:

If you are reaching up to get something – like a book off a shelf – you can only reach so far if you don't spiral. A spiral is just a way of creating a longer line through the body, because there is more space than if we just work up and down and side to side. There is life in the spiral: if you look at plants and nature, everything is built from spirals, things rarely just grow up, there is a curving and a twisting.[47]

High Release

As well as the three fundamentals there is also an action called *high release* or *high lift*. High release, or high lift, is a development and increase of Release into a hyperextension of the upper spine. The action lifts the breast bone up, opens the chest, and tilts

Fig. 41: Seated with the feet together in high release. Graham class taught by Geneviève Grady, featuring dancers Alice Lovrinic, Anna Broome, Federica Bertani and Laure Dubanet; Trinity Laban Conservatoire of Music and Dance, London. JAMES KEATES

the head back. It is usually done with an inhalation, so the lungs support the lifting in the chest and balance the weight of the skull. High release can be combined with spiral so the head is turned and the lower spine rotated as the chest lifts.

TECHNICAL VOCABULARY

Contraction, release and spiral centre the movement of the body in the torso between the hips and shoulders. The torso moves first, and the legs and arms become gesturing limbs, their movement instigated by motion in the torso. Thus, movement is from the centre of the body out, as Agnes De Mille describes: '…arms and legs, accordingly, were not lifted or lowered; they were driven in propulsion, and propulsion that was quite visible.'[48]

A Graham class starts sitting on the floor, emphasizing a connection to the ground; the movement of the torso is through the use of contraction, release and spiral, all of which involve movement of the spine and pelvis. As the pelvis is the primary support structure for the first part of the Graham class rather than the feet, the pelvis becomes the foundation for the movement in the technique.

Understanding the structure of the pelvis and how it moves and relates to the spine can be really useful knowledge to support the technique. Being aware of the bony landmarks of the pelvis can help with the internal sensing of these, and how they move. Touch can facilitate this awareness – when sitting, feeling contact between the bony landmarks and the floor, such as the sitting bones or ischia (sometimes referred to as the feet of the pelvis); feeling the front of the iliac crests when lying prone on the belly; and the sacrum when lying supine on the back (*see* Figures 34 and 39).

Touch with the hands can help identify the hip sockets, the pubic synthesis, and how the ilia meet the sacrum at the sacroiliac joints. Touch with the hands can also help to feel the movement of the bones, as the sacrum and ilia move in relation to each other at the sacroiliac joints, and you can feel how this moves the sitting bones towards or away from each other.

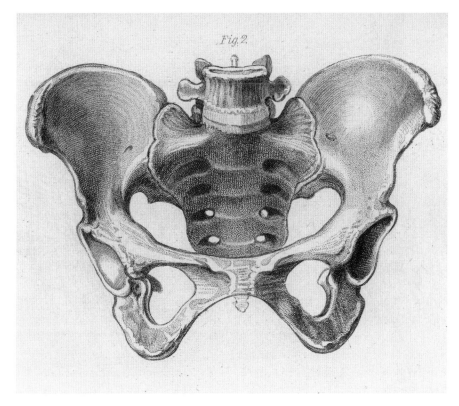

Fig.2.

Fig. 42: Bones of the pelvis. WELLCOME LIBRARY, LONDON

Fig. 43: Simple contractions. Graham class taught by Geneviève Grady, featuring dancers Alice Lovrinic, Anna Broome, Federica Bertani and Laure Dubanet; Trinity Laban Conservatoire of Music and Dance, London. JAMES KEATES

In the floor exercises the torso initiates the action from the lower belly, the pelvic floor muscles and the pelvis, and then the spine responds, and maybe the arms and/or legs, and/or the head. There is often a sense of reaching a place – reaching the depth of contraction, reaching full extension of the torso on the release, reaching the spiral – so there are destinations to seek as physical experiences. But these fundamental actions are activities of change, not positions: you move into contraction and into release.

To facilitate an experiential process of how a destination can be moved towards, Graham teacher Geneviève Grady sometimes uses a slower, student-led process of exploring moving into contraction, release and high release as an introductory exercise, in which the process of moving and the sensations of the body in that motion are emphasized before faster and more percussive initiation is approached. Sarah Sule-

manji describes a seated exploration of the breath that she uses with her students:

We will be working with the breath as a starting point. I explain to them that this is our centre, right down in the pelvis in between the hip bones, and I get them to visualize the breath, and take a really big breath in and to visualize the breath as a material thing, as a material object they are taking into the body. So as they breathe in they are filling up their torso from right down in the base of the spine, up the body, and then as they exhale, as something comes out of us, then we get smaller and the breath is emptying. So it is that constant filling up and expanding and then emptying.[49]

Structured sitting exercises have particular use of the arms and legs, and the spatial reach of the limb actions increases through the order of the

Fig. 44: Self-practice. Graham class taught by Geneviève Grady, featuring dancers Kirbie Franks, Rosemary Copp and Anna Broome; Trinity Laban Conservatoire of Music and Dance, London. JAMES KEATES

exercises. When sitting with the soles of the feet together, the hands are placed on the shin bones in a loose grip (*see* Figure 43). When the ankles are crossed there can be a curve of the arms sideways and down from the shoulders, facilitated by the fingertips touching the floor and the elbows held outwards from the ribcage. The touch on the floor is light, as the support for the arms comes from a widening of the back, not the ground, showing again that the floor is used but there is no yielding or dropping of weight.

This arm shaping is repeated in standing work, so the arms are held slightly out from the body with space visible between the inner surface of the arms and the torso, with the palms facing inwards. This placement, which is often described as 'space in the armpits', requires a broadening of the upper back and thus an active sensation in the upper body, particularly under the shoulder blades and in the chest. This engagement comes from the lungs, and supports the feeling

of engaged relationship between the arms and the torso, and also a bound flow in the expression of the upper body (*see* 'Dynamics' below).

The fingertips touching the floor can also be reiterated in the legs, with the toes lightly touching the floor when sitting with the ankles crossed. This means that the weight is carried in the pelvis with some weight balancing on the outside of the little toe metatarsal. This position for the legs is traditionally used in the *breathings* and the *simple spirals* exercises. Simple spirals start with the arms lengthened and touching the knees with the palms down, creating lines and angles in the shaping. (Videos of Graham Technique can be found through the school website: marthagraham.edu, which links to YouTube.) Tutors may start the exploration of the physical changes in the torso in different leg positions to enable the depth of motion of the contraction and the supportive expansion of the release, before adding particular shaping in the limbs.

Exercises such as *openings* and *long leans* then use large opening actions in the limbs, which are still initiated by contraction, release, spiral and high release. In the technique there is a shaping in the hands that can be used, which is called *cupped hands*. This is a backward fold in the wrist and a simultaneous forward fold in the knuckle joints of the fingers, creating a concave shape in the hand, as if holding an object. A shaping of space is created, which in choreological practice is called *spatial* tension.[50]

In the exercise *pleadings*, which starts lying on the back supine, a contraction brings the shoulders off the floor and bends the knees (see Figure 47). The arms remain long and extended along the sides of the body, but the cupped hands allow the heel of the hands to pull forwards. As the exercise progresses, the pull from the heels of the hands facilitates a deepening of the contraction and an increased lifting off the floor. Geneviève Grady describes this as follows:

> In the pleading the heels of the hands are drawing the shoulder blades forward so the sternum and heart can soften against that drawing forward. The deep opening of the back and the softening of the sternum and the deep work of the pelvic floor with the lift and hollowing out through the front... one feeds the other. [51]

Contraction and release are explored in different orientations to gravity, and with different points of support in the body. The first point of support is the base of the pelvis – the sitting bones – but the support then becomes the back and lower back (*pleadings*), the knees (exercise on 6), and the feet (tendus, extensions/batement, triplets, jumps). In sitting, the torso between the hips and the shoulders becomes the primary movement,

Fig. 45: Pleadings. Graham class taught by Geneviève Grady, featuring dancers Mitchell Davis and Anna Broome; Trinity Laban Conservatoire of Music and Dance, London. JAMES KEATES

Fig. 46: Supporting on the shoulders. Graham class taught by Geneviève Grady, featuring dancers Federica Bertani, Mitchell Davis, Jeanne Delévaque and Laure Dubanet; Trinity Laban Conservatoire of Music and Dance, London. JAMES KEATES

and the belly becomes the centre of motion, which then expands outwards through the limbs into space. This connection from the belly to the peripheries then becomes fundamental to the technique and movement, and energy radiates out from or into this centre, creating closing and opening patterns. Often these patterns are fully expressed with the contraction drawing either the whole body or at least the full energy into the centre, and then the opening completing in full extension of the limbs.

ACTION

Because the centre to periphery bodily motion is so prevalent in the technique, the actions of *opening* and *closing* are, of course, highly significant. These actions relate the use of the body to an attitude to space as an integrated phenomenon. The opening to space is in the lungs and belly as well as through the limbs, and projected out into the environment. The inward energy of closing draws the attention inwards to the torso, both sensorial for the dancer

Fig. 47: Contraction with forward pull through the arms. Graham class taught by Geneviève Grady, featuring dancers Mitchell Davis and Laure Dubanet; Trinity Laban Conservatoire of Music and Dance, London.

JAMES KEATES

and visibly for the perceiver. There is a constant flux in these actions through the movement.

At times the closing energy can be predominant, such as in the exercise *pleadings*, where the release of contraction brings the body to a more neutral lengthening, rather than a projected one; sometimes there is an equality between the opening and closing, such as in *deep stretches*; sometimes the opening is more emphasized, such as during travelling steps when the closing can be a brief change in the shift of weight between large opening actions.

The spiral, too, is an opening rather than a twist, due to the orientation of the head and the spatial projection of the focus beyond the forward shoulder, as well as how the spiral instigates openings of the limbs into space. Gestures of the limbs tend to be extensions of the torso action either with a rotating action with the drawing in or opening out, or with an extension into space from the centre. Although the class structure incorporates tendus (extensions of the legs at a low level in the dimensions forwards/backwards, right/left), these are done with a spiral in the torso, so the leg becomes a part of the cross-lateral closing or opening.

NAMED POSITIONS

There are named body positions in the technique, such as *fourth position* and *pretzel* (*see* Figure 48), which are moved into and out of with contraction, spiral and release. Pretzel is a tightly closed sitting position with one bent leg crossed over the other, and the body curved and wrapped over the legs; this position requires a certain degree of range of motion in the hips.

Fourth position is a sitting position in which one leg is turned inwards from the hip and bent so that the foot points backwards and is close to the pelvis, whereas the other leg is turned out and bent in front of the body with the weight on the little toe side of the foot. This position also demands a certain degree of range in the hip joints that is not always available to those starting the technique. Geneviève Grady speaks of only using 'the class choreography and exercises that are accessible to the group as a whole, and then use those in a way that exposes everyone to the potential of their body, and then explore more codified material as the students' ability increases.'[52]

She also talks about starting to work on some exercises in parallel, sitting on the shins so students can explore the action of spiralling, and the notion of two sides of the body wrapping around the core before using that spiralling action from fourth position or sitting with ankles crossed.

TRANSFERENCE OF WEIGHT

In moving between named positions there is another action of particular significance in the technique, *transference of weight*. Shifting the weight in Graham Technique is purposeful and without hesitation. Even in seated exercises there can be a definitive shift of the weight between different points of support. For example, there is a shift of weight into a forward tilt of the torso in release, which can be called a *pitch*. This

Fig. 48: Pretzel. Graham class taught by Geneviève Grady, featuring dancers Anna Broome, Pagan Hunt, Kirbie Franks, Alice Lovrinic and Natalya Smith; Trinity Laban Conservatoire of Music and Dance, London. JAMES KEATES

action moves the support of the weight of the body forwards into the legs as the body leans forwards; even if the sitting bones remain touching the floor, the shift in the transference of weight is visible.

In *turns around the back* that starts from fourth position, the transference of weight from the sitting bones to the side of the top of one thigh, and the spiral twist in the torso that results from that, is made visible even with a slow and sustained speed (*see* Figure 39). Shifts from one surface of the pelvis to another, and from the feet to the pelvis, the pelvis to the back, and the pelvis to the knees, are highlighted features in the movement language.

There are also actions called *falls*, which are very large leaning actions into transferences of weight. These start as leans in the torso, which lead to a controlled shift on to a new supporting surface. The control comes from the fact that the centre of gravity in the pelvis actually stays over the centre of support all the way through the action.[53] This trans-forms the action from the usual definition of a fall, which involves a loss of equilibrium and a letting go of weight into gravity, into a controlled action that involves moving down in the direction of gravity with the weight leading. A fall can be at various speeds. As Geneviève Grady says: '...a fall can be slower than gravity or quicker than gravity.'[54]

If a fall is from standing, and particularly if it is sustained, it is the reaching out and balancing effect of the limbs in different directions (what can be termed in choreological practice the *spatial scaffolding*) that allows for the extreme angle of the lean and the weight to lead the action but with a control of speed. The fall is then caught with a new supporting surface so sometimes the torso remains off the floor. Even if the fall is on to the back, there is no giving in to the ground at the end of the fall; instead there can be a rebounding of the energy, like a ball hitting a wall and rebounding off, which leads to a new transference of weight.

Fig. 49: Pitch turn. Graham class taught by Geneviève Grady, featuring dancers Anna Broome, Kirbie Franks, Jeanne Delévaque and Federica Bertani; Trinity Laban Conservatoire of Music and Dance, London. JAMES KEATES

There are *Graham walks*, which are turned out forward or backward steps in which the whole body is propelled forwards on to a new support from the standing foot pushing off the floor. In the centre, Graham walks can involve a round movement of the leg (called a *ronde de jambe à terre* in ballet), in which the toe travels on a peripheral path (around the outside) on the floor to achieve the forward or backward direction in preparation for the weight transference. As the leg circles the torso spirals in opposition, and the gaze travels with the spiral so that the dancer scans the horizon.

Walks can also be done as travelling actions. Travelling actions are often done towards the end of a class, as steps from the back (upstage) corner of the space across to the opposite front (downstage) corner. One of the main travelling steps is the *triplet*. The triplet is a set of three large, forward steps: the first step is low level on to a bent leg, and the next two steps are high level on the balls of the feet. The triplet uses the spiral in the torso, which can act as an instigator for the action. The torso can twist to the right on an upbeat, and then the weight shifts forwards on to the right foot; the spiral then stays during the two high-level steps. Because the first step is on the leg that opposes the direction of the twist, it almost feels as if the first step crosses the body.

TRIPLET

A triplet is a travelling action of three steps in one movement phrase. The word 'triplet' is also used in music but is rhythmically differ-ent. In music a triplet is one beat (or crochet) divided into three equal parts. In dance, a triplet is a movement phrase of three move-ments on three beats and is thus usually done to a three-quarter time signature.

JUMPS AND TURNS

There are also turns and jumps in the technical vocabulary, and each action is large and committed and visible. Turns can be sustained or very fast, and can be done with a strong accent, emphasizing the initiation. Turns are often initiated with spirals in the torso that lead into the direction of turning, which can be done upright with the torso in the vertical, but also with the torso leaning. A particular example of this is the *pitch turn*, where the torso is pitched forwards and down with enough spiral to propel the body around as the gesturing leg lifts up and back (*see* Figure 49). Turns can be done on the feet, on the hips, and on the knees. They are generally less than two turns, with a small one-eighth turn (such as the shift on to one hip in a pleading) being as significant in performance as one and a quarter turns (such as a pitch turn).

Jumps are various, large and can combine with opening and closing actions. *Sparkles* is the name given to a jump with an opening in which a hop on one foot is done with a spiral in the torso and a reaching out from the centre with both arms lifting and the gesturing leg extending behind. There is a standing action called a bison, which is also done as a leap (*see* Figure 59). Bison is a contraction with all the limbs bent, where the torso moves forwards over the front leg and thus becomes a closing action. As a leap the focus remains forwards and pulls the body forwards in space, even in a closed action.

SPACE

In this technique there is a clarity in the spatial energy of the body, as everything is part of the action. The entire body is involved in the movement, as the energy flows from the centre of the lower belly out to the peripheries and back again. The sense of reaching out from the centre creates movement that is expansive in space. Movements that extend into the limbs can be very large, and shifts of weight are big. Lines and curves in the limbs are created as an extension of the energy from the torso. The facing of the palms, and thus the rotation of the arms, can change the shaping of the arms in relation to the

Fig. 50: Reach into space. Graham class taught by Geneviève Grady, featuring dancers Anna Broome, Pagan Hunt, Kirbie Franks, Alice Lovrinic and Natalya Smith; Trinity Laban Conservatoire of Music and Dance, London. JAMES KEATES

torso. Straight, curved or angular positions of the arms arise from flexion in the joints – elbows, wrists and knuckles.

In exercises the arms have a clear starting shape, which then change with the actions of the torso. In one seated exercise, *deep stretches*, there are variations in which the arms can start in different positions and then change with the torso changes. In one variation the arms start in a diamond shape around the head with the elbows bent at about ninety degrees and the palms facing forwards:

- On the contraction the elbows are brought forwards in front of the chest with the palms facing towards the head, so there is an inward rotation of the arms matching the inward feeling in the belly, which allows the shoulder blades to open and the thoracic spine to curve
- On the release, the arms then return to the diamond shape as the chest opens with the lengthening of the spine

Another angular shape can be found in standing

Fig. 51: Second position plié with open arms. Graham class taught by Geneviève Grady, featuring dancers Mitchell Davis, Pagan Hunt, Anna Broome, Kirby Franks, Rosemary Copp, Jeanne Delévaque and Alice Lovrinic; Trinity Laban Conservatoire of Music and Dance, London. JAMES KEATES

work, when all the limbs are bent with one leg lifted behind with the ankle flexed, and the arms with bent elbows and wrists held out from the body horizontal to the floor. Curved shaping in the arms can be seen in Figure 51, when a long, open, uplifted curve expands the uplifted energy in the upper torso.

The spiral creates use of the forward diagonal directions as the shoulder line orientates to one forward diagonal and the face to the opposite forward diagonal. The sitting exercises also make use of the forward diagonal as directions for the legs and torso, although there is no set location, and the individual must discover their own optimal placement.

SPATIAL PROJECTION

Extending out from the centre often leads to *spatial projection*,[55] which is the virtual image of extension beyond the body and out into space. The range of the extension into space is facilitated by the clarity of connection between the limbs and the body centre, but is developed to create a spatial energy that can project beyond the body. Spatial projection is a virtual energy that extends beyond the body into space: the line or curve of energy in space only exists in the mind of the perceiver, but is generated by the commitment of the dancer in creating an expressive virtual force. The performer creates an illusion through the clarity of their physical intention in terms of energetic commitment in the body,

Fig. 52: Spatial projection. Graham class taught by Geneviève Grady, featuring dancers Federica Bertani and Laure Dubanet; Trinity Laban Conservatoire of Music and Dance, London. JAMES KEATES

particularly in terms of the size of the movement, and spatial attention.

'Projection' is a word often used in performance disciplines, but can often refer to energy in the face or voice, directed towards the audience, or alternatively to the idea of character or personality projection. In Graham this virtual projection of energy beyond the body limits can be created with any part of the body, or several at once. In the floor exercise *long leans*, the arms extend from, and emphasize the lean and the spiral of the torso towards a high forward diagonal location. The directing of the face and eyes to look beyond the reach of the arm supports the spatial projection. Thus, the complexity of the spiral in the torso and the extending out, leads to a multifaceted sensorial experience, but a simple and direct spatial energy through the direction of the gaze which creates a spatial clarity. Often the direction of the gaze becomes the visibly dominant feature of this energetic projection. Sarah Sulemanji describes this as the face 'winning' in the expansion of energy from the centre through the peripheries. Thus, the orientation of the face can drive the direction of the movement through space, particularly in locomotion.

For example, a *tilt* is an action in Graham where the weight is supported on one leg with the torso tilted up and high to one side, the free leg lifted to the other side, and the arms extended sideways out from the shoulders (see Figure 53). The face is orientated over the standing leg with the gaze extended beyond the arm. The strength of the direction of the gaze can pull the weight after it, leading to a pull off balance for the centre of gravity in the pelvis. This causes a quick step across the original standing leg to regain balance, and then a motion into a repeat of the tilt. Thus, the gaze can be the initiator of the shifting of weight and creates travelling through space, as was described above in bison jumps.

Fig. 53: Graham class taught by Geneviève Grady, featuring dancers Mitchell Davis, Alice Lovrinic, Rosemary Copp and Jessy MacKay; Trinity Laban Conservatoire of Music and Dance, London. JAMES KEATES

DYNAMICS

EMOTIONAL RESONANCE

Armitage (1966) states that Graham's movement language is the result of emotional experiences that found channels through the movement she evolved. Martin in 1937 stated that Graham's choreography 'is essentially dealing in abstractions, yet they are somehow so terrifically energized that the effect is one of sweeping emotion'.[56] Hargrave (1937) says of Martha Graham that 'her true importance lies in the projection of an emotional force'.[57]

In the technique class there is no necessity to portray a defined emotion (happy, sad, angry) – rather, the sense of emotional resonance arises from the visceral energy in the fundamental principles of the form and the use of time. The word 'visceral' relates to both the large internal organs of the body (the heart, lungs, stomach, liver, intestines), and to emotional feeling and reaction. The organs are the site of our basic emotional state. Nerve endings in the fascial connective tissues around and in between the organs send messages to the brain about the condition of the body: this is known as interoception.[58] Feelings such as hunger arise in this way: thus the organs are connected to our fundamental emotional responses.

When the breath and movement of the torso act as initiators, then this underlying emotive connection is integrated with, and supports, our movement in space. So there is a matching of movement intention through the layers of the body. This leads to a fuller and clear expression in the body. The movement does not need to express emotion: there is an emotional subtext to every movement because of the integration of organ energy to movement of the torso and limbs. In Laban Movement Analysis (LMA), which evolved from Rudolf Laban's research through the work of Irmgard Bartenieff and Peggy Hackney, this is known as *shape flow*: the constant flux of shaping deep in the body through the breath, and how that is expressed in actions in space. The energy and expression from the organs are also an important part of Bonnie Bainbridge Cohen's Body Mind Centering (BMC).

Fig. 54: Using the breath to initiate the contraction. Graham class taught by Geneviève Grady, featuring dancers Laure Dubanet and Jeanne Delévaque; Trinity Laban Conservatoire of Music and Dance, London. JAMES KEATES

In Graham Technique the contraction moves beyond the flux of breathing into a fuller bodily action that heightens the connection to the organs through a deep squeezing and releasing. The speed of the contraction can then shift the resonance from a sudden reaction to a more sensual flow.

IMAGERY

This emotional connection to moving is then developed through the use of imagery. Imagery engages the dancers' imagination and emotional being into the act of performance to support the intention behind the movement. The imagery can vary from teacher to teacher but is used to allow the students' imagination to support the dynamic qualities and performance mode desired. Agnes De Mille (1991) says that:

Martha talked in enlightened poetry. Sometimes the explanations had very little to do with the work at hand...but they gave an oblique insight into what she was feeling. Her remarks were sometimes cryptic, generally brief...and often humorous, lightning quick in their revelation and lightning powerful in their striking force.

Geneviève Grady uses imagery from our connection to nature – earth, blood and trees – to engage her students with a sense of the ground, and growing up away from it with different degrees of strength. Sarah Sulemanji speaks of images to connect to space with intention such as:

...lifting up out of the box for opening, moving through a high viscous liquid so you can create some kind of resistance, feeling the sunlight on your face, looking out over the horizon. In Graham and Graham work there is that real opportunity to explore expressionism, there is a real emotive quality and a way of performing...from the inside out, from how we are feeling.[59]

FLOW

The feeling of moving viscerally from the organs in the belly lends itself to use of the *flow motion factor* (*see* Chapter 2). Rudolf Laban associated flow with feeling and emotion. Flow has two polarities: *bound* and *free*. Laban said 'The flow of movement is bound when the feel of it takes an inward direction',[60] and there is, then, a resistance to gravity and space rather than a giving in. The muscular energy around the organs in Graham Technique brings both an emotional force to the movement language and a bound flow dynamic energy.

Bound flow is not stiffness, but a sense of motion that does not release energy away from the body. There is a flow of energy, but it is contained within the skin, so even though the body may extend into space and spatial projection can be created, there is no blurring of boundaries between performer and space: there is no giving in to space or to gravity. The spatial projection comes from a centre, and that centre is the person who does not release any of

ABOVE: **Fig. 55: Students at Trinity Laban Conservatoire of Music and Dance performing the Graham repertoire.** TRINITY LABAN © KYLE STEVENSON

RIGHT: **Fig. 56: Geneviève Grady teaching a Graham class, featuring dancers Anna Broome, Federica Bertani, Mitchell Davis, Pagan Hunt and Rosemary Copp; Trinity Laban Conservatoire of Music and Dance, London.** JAMES KEATES

their power. Geneviève Grady describes this in relation to the mode of performance: she says, '…it is a sense of power that is still inviting the audience in. I have made myself available to you without giving up my autonomy.'[61]

POWER

The sense of personal power in this dance form is also a particular feature of the dynamics. A strong energy is visible. There is a connection to the ground in Graham Technique, but that does not lead to a heavy expression: rather, there is a strong connection to the floor and a sense of pushing off the floor. It is the floor that allows for a pushing away from the ground, creating a vertical energy from the floor up.

This upward lift is part of contraction, release, high release and spiral, and thus pervades all the action.

This press off the floor can also be seen in Graham walks, in which the back foot pushes off the ground to propel the body forwards on to the front foot. This strength of press can also be seen in Graham jumps, which are high and powerful: as Graham dancer Frieda Flier said: 'You were resisting the floor. And the way you jumped, you bounced away from the floor.'[62] This strength for jumping arises from the strong pelvic floor that develops in the floor work, and the use of the contraction as the initiation for movement.

There can be a feeling of empowerment in this use of strong energy, and this is expressed very clearly in the gaze, when the eyes look out boldly to the edges of the space or beyond. The sense of looking beyond the space is also an act of engaging the imagination. It sets up a relationship to space that is challenging and outward – images of the pioneer, the warrior, can be associated with Graham's choreography and technique. If you try a strong and outward gaze coupled with a bound inward energy in the belly around the lower organs, you should find the sensibility of the Graham performance mode. It was described that Graham 'looks across the stage, and the boundaries of theatre dissolve into frightening distance.'[63]

The very deliberate and controlled shape changing in the torso, as well as the core peripheral connection, creates a clarity in the shaping in the results of action. The spatial form is purposeful and without hesitation. Despite the fact that the shaping of the body can be curved, there is a clarity of directing the body in space: there is no spatial indulgence. This can create a boldness, a fearless expression when combined with strong energy. In Laban theory, when the motion factors space (direct–indirect) and force (strong–light) combine, the result is a dynamic state known as *stable*.[64]

Stable that results from an expression of a *strong* force energy, with attention to *direct* spatial clarity, can create a strong presence, like a warrior. Laban and Ullmann describe stable as 'solid and powerful'.[65] The warrior's movements are powerful and

purposeful, and can be done at great speed. Fettes describes stable as: 'A commanding demonstration of a "bold resolve".'[66] Thus the dynamics show an absolute commitment to each movement. Graham is said to have said: 'You attack dance as "Now!" Not what it will develop into, not what I have done – (but) what I am doing.'[67] There can be a feeling of empowerment in this use of a directed strong energy, which is expressed very clearly in the gaze.

SPELL DRIVE

When bound flow and strong force are combined, this can create a full physical sensation of the motion of the body. When flow qualities and force qualities combine with attention to space through clear shaping – such as the shaping of the spine in contraction and release, and spatial energy such as the spatial projection of the gaze – Laban theory terms this *spell drive*.[68] Fettes describes spell drive as when someone appears 'to inhabit an eternal world, one that exhibits no past and no future, and that therefore resembles the condition of the gods themselves.'[69]

This resonates with comments about Graham's choreography, in that her characters are often described as *archetypal*, which means they are strong examples of particular types of persons. *The Cambridge Dictionary* defines this as 'a typical example of something, or the original model of something from which others are copied'. Many of her characters are taken from Greek mythology and so are ancient representations of societal roles and types of personalities – but despite the fact that her movement language was highly influenced by Asian dance forms and movement practices, her characters were often derived from European or Colonial American narratives.

PASSION DRIVE

When flow qualities and force qualities combine with attention to the motion factor time, through sudden actions such as percussive contractions, Laban theory terms this *passion drive*, and describes it as when 'bodily actions are particularly expressive of emotion and feeling'.[70] Fettes et al. describe passion

Fig. 57: Contraction with legs extended. Graham class taught by Geneviève Grady, featuring dancers Mitchell Davis and Anna Broome; Trinity Laban Conservatoire of Music and Dance, London. JAMES KEATES

drive as a 'constructing and destroying' energy; they continue: '[passion is] the absence of thinking, attending and space', and they add to this description using the terms 'overpowering' and 'irradiant'.[71]

Martha Graham was known as a passionate performer, and the technique can be taught in this way. The physical embodiment of the dynamic qualities prevents this passion from being affectation or mimicry, but rather situates it in the substance of the moving body as an emotive and empowered expression. The expression comes not from the face, but from the kinaesthetic experience of the powerful physicality. Graham as a performer was said to be 'completely honest and direct'.[72] Martin describes Martha Graham's performance in 1937 thus: 'She boils down her moods and movements until they are devoid of all extraneous substances and are concentrated to the highest degree.'[73]

RELATIONSHIPS

In Graham's choreography the relationship to the viewer is one of creating expressive statements, and the audience was the direction for that expression. Her work was situated in the proscenium arch theatre, where the audience is on one side of the performance space, with the auditorium extending away from the stage into darkness. The sight lines for the audience's view influenced the construction of the choreography, in that there is a clear front, and arrangements of the performers have a direct relationship to that front.

This is clearly presented in the works *Heretic* and *Primitive Mysteries* (*see* Figure 32), where the black-clothed ensemble creates a shape around the white-clad central dancer, framing the soloist for the audience. The audience's attention was also directed specifically at the action, with no conflict for attention. Stillness was used as a device to clearly shift the audience's focus from one performer or group to another performer or group on the stage. This can be seen in the work *Night Journey* (1947, based on the story of Oedipus), when the focus moves from Oedipus and his mother Jocasta, the soothsayer and the group of attendants.

Due to this clarity of focus, each movement is a statement ready to be viewed: thus each movement in the technique is a statement – it is action executed

Fig. 58: Lunge position. Graham class taught by Geneviève Grady, featuring dancers Rosemary Copp and Pagan Hunt; Trinity Laban Conservatoire of Music and Dance, London. JAMES KEATES

with the whole body with a purposefulness and control. The body relationship of the centre-periphery connection, and the open and closing patterns, are the primary intra-personal (within the self) relationship structures. The visceral energy that this can facilitate, coupled with emotive imagery, can then produce an emotional resonance to these action statements.

The relationship to space is also significant both in terms of the size of motion and the use of projection, but also in relation to the floor because of the low level for a lot of the movement within the technique, as well as how different areas of the body become the base of support. The dancer is in control and in charge of the movement of their body and the use of space. There is a correctness to the form.

Despite this requirement for accuracy, the movement should be performed with a supple aliveness rather than a rigidity. The dancer therefore has to rise to the challenge of taking ownership of their movement, and must find an emotional strength to do this. There is a boldness that can arise from a contending energy – an energy that boldly places self in space.

Traditionally all dance technique training was taught in quite an authoritarian way, with the teacher as the ultimate authority figure who must be obeyed and appeased. A high discipline was demanded, and the teacher could be an intimidating figure who could punish as well as praise. Teaching has changed significantly in recent decades, and a more caring, student valuing and nurturing attitude is practised. However, the idea that you can rise to meet a powerful presence in an empowered way still pervades the imagery of the practice.

Geneviève Grady describes her teacher, Pearl Lang, who worked under Graham herself in the Graham company, and was the first to replace Graham in performing the soloist roles, as beautiful but terrifying:

> 'She could be brutally honest and uncompromising, and I suppose that is partly why I trusted her, that and her undeniable history. I felt seen; there was no hiding from her, and therefore there was no hiding from myself.'

There was a requirement to bring your whole self to the practice, which was palpable as 'there was no other way than you stepping forward into this moment'.[74]

For Geneviève Grady this became a place of personal empowerment, and that sensibility imbues her student-centred teaching practice. She states that her students 'understand that the emotional is a part of [the practice]; they can see it in my body when I demonstrate. But the opening up of the body is such a challenging, terrifying thing sometimes.'[75] Thus each dancer must find their own physical energy, power and stamina.

Fig. 59: Graham class taught by Geneviève Grady, featuring dancers Mitchell Davis and Alice Lovrinic; Trinity Laban Conservatoire of Music and Dance, London. JAMES KEATES

MUSIC AND SOUND

In the class, each dancer is separate within their own kinespheric space. However, due to the clarity and structure of the movement, when performed to set time structures, there can be a strong unison in the performance of exercises, creating an overall collective unity which can provide a sense of group support. The floor exercises in the technique, when taught following the set forms, have set counts and phrasing. Through this, different time signatures and musical structures are utilized.

At times these musical structures can change even within an exercise, such as in the exercise pleadings. In pleadings the duration of a phrase of movement extends and develops with each repetition: the first pleadings are on four counts, but then extend to six counts or ten counts. Some exercises are known by the time signature, such as *exercise on 6* which is a kneeling exercise, and *breathings on 3 and 4*. In this way the accompaniment and movement are integrated, and the breath pattern follows the musical pulse and time signature.

In this way the accompaniment and movement are integrated and there is the possibility of 'explor-

Fig. 60: Jumps. Graham class taught by Geneviève Grady, featuring dancer Anna Broome; Trinity Laban Conservatoire of Music and Dance, London. JAMES KEATES

Fig. 61: Tilt on the floor. Graham class taught by Geneviève Grady, featuring dancers Mitchell Davis and Laure Dubanet; Trinity Laban Conservatoire of Music and Dance, London. JAMES KEATES

Fig. 62: Seated practice. Graham class taught by Geneviève Grady, featuring dancers Jessy MacKay, Alice Lovrinic, Anna Broome, Federica Bertani, Mitchell Davis, Natalya Smith, Pagan Hunt, Rosemary Copp, Kirbie Franks, Jeanne Delévaque and Laure Dubanet; Trinity Laban Conservatoire of Music and Dance, London. JAMES KEATES

GENEVIÈVE GRADY'S CONSIDERATIONS

I am free to not teach to a syllabus, but I do still feel a clear responsibility toward the traditional material. We need to know where we are coming from, not merely in service of the past, but because the technique exists for us now as a nuanced and intelligent movement system within which many things are possible. I have to ask myself, why do I believe this technique has the potential to serve the needs of the contemporary dancer? I answer the question through the practice of teaching. I incorporate yoga or contemporary movement material relevant to the connection between breath, spine, space, and psyche but maintain context for the dancer by declaring what of the material is traditional Graham and in what ways the non-traditional material supports it. A lot of what stylistically makes it Graham has to do with initiation and our embodied emotional response. Ultimately, it is a playground toward self-knowledge. Over a number of weeks, with a class we move towards only Graham syllabus material. [78]

SARAH SULEMANJI'S CONSIDERATIONS

I do use a relatively traditional framework when it comes to class. We have one hour and a half classes, so we work on the floor for half an hour, we work in the centre for half an hour, we travel across the space. What I do in that is quite free, I switch around and I change a lot with what I do. I think it is very important that they [the students] are in a place where they can pick up lots of different movement material, where they are able to really see that it is those fundamental principles that we are working with, that are important. How they are using the back, how they can come from up to going down, what those fundamental things are, and doing that in lots and lots of different ways as opposed to doing that in just one way. It is not about just doing structures, there are some exercises, yes, we do lot of breathings on the floor, but we will do them in lots of different ways, using the back, using the arms. [79]

ing the relationship of breath to metric time'. [76] Movement sequences are usually counted or follow a pulse. Phrases can be quite fast paced, especially travelling and jumping phrases, so the pulse drives the energy of the movement.

STRUCTURES OF A CLASS

At the Graham School there is a structure and order to the set exercises:

1. Breathings
2. Bounces
3. Simple spiral
4. Long leans
5. Spiral turns
6. Exercise on 6
7. Pliés
8. Contraction side to side
9. Walks
10. Triplet
11. Step draw
12. Travelling jumps

Teachers working in different contexts may follow this order of exercises, or use it as a template and adapt to the groups and context they are teaching in. When approaching teaching Graham Technique, Geneviève Grady asks herself 'how does it best serve us, and how can we move forwards with it, without losing what it is?' [77]

CHAPTER 4

CUNNINGHAM TECHNIQUE

BACKGROUND AND PRINCIPLES

Cunningham Technique was devised by the choreographer Merce Cunningham to support his choreographic work. Merce Cunningham was an American dancer and choreographer whose career spanned seventy years. He was born in Centralia, Washington, USA, in 1919, and starting dancing at the age of twelve; he then attended the Cornish Institute of Fine and Allied Arts (now the Cornish College of the Arts) in Seattle. In 1939 he joined the Graham Company, being only the second man to do so. Cunningham danced for Martha Graham for five years, during which time he started to explore his own independent choreographic practice, presenting his first work with composer John Cage in New York in 1944. In 1953 he established his own company, Merce Cunningham and Dancers; later this name was changed to the Merce Cunningham Dance Company.

'Merce Cunningham changed the way a generation or more of dancers and spectators thinks about dancing.'[80] His work took inspiration from current artistic thinking and innovation of the time, and he drew in collaborators who exemplified those ideas. Cunningham's collaborators included composers John Cage, David Tudor, David Behrman, Christian Wolff and La Monte Young, and visual artists Robert Rauschenberg, Jasper Johns and Andy Warhol.[81]

Cunningham's artistic practice developed from a desire to break away from certain beliefs that were assumed fundamental to dance as a performance art. He stated: 'I used to be told that you see the centre of the space as the most important: that it was the centre of interest. But in many modern paintings this was not the case, and the sense of space was different.' He then asked himself the question: 'What if...you decide to make any point on the stage equally interesting?'[82] Because Cunningham's choreography reformulates conventional stage space,[83] his work then represented and embodied a new democratized use of space, as the action could happen in any part of the performance space and with any orientation.

Initially, many performances of his early work were outside conventional theatre settings, in venues such as college gyms which did not have an established viewpoint, something which is literally built into the architecture of the proscenium arch theatre. Dancers in his work could face in any direction with equal energy, rather than predominantly facing the direction of the audience, or projecting energy towards the audience. This alteration in the relationship to 'front' had the effect of equalizing the energy in all surfaces of the body. Thus, Cunningham's use of the body exemplified his use of space: there is a democratization of the body, as every part and every surface is equally significant. Cunningham stated: 'You can see a person not just from the front, but from any side with equal interest.'[84]

Cunningham's work is also infamous for his use of music. Rather than using music as an inspirational source for movement creation (like Isadora Duncan), or as structural support and for definition of the choreography (like Graham), Cunningham separates the dance from the sound score so they act like independent voices in a work. He was exposed to the ideas of the radical composer John Cage at the Cornish School when Cunningham

Fig. 63: Merce Cunningham and dancers, 16 April 1919–26 July 2009. WIKIMEDIA COMMONS

Fig. 64: Trinity Laban students performing in a Cunningham event re-created by Daniel Squire, 20–21 June 2017. TRINITY LABAN COPYRIGHT JAMES KEATES

was a student and Cage was on the faculty. Their later collaboration led them to explore a co-existent music/dance relationship, where the movement and sound happen simultaneously in performance, but with no intentional direct correlation.[85]

This meant that the dancers had to feel the time structure of the movement itself, as it was not associated with musical narrative: this focused attention on the performance of the movement in the time of the body in action. The choreography does not have any intentional expressive use of time – there is no crescendo, no explosive gestures as in Graham, no use of the organic rhythmic processes of letting go in gravity to find fall and recovery or swing, as in Humphrey Limon Technique. There are changes in speed and duration of movements, but

Fig. 65: Cunningham class taught by Gary Lambert, with dancers Georgia Heighway, Samantha Furnival, Sophie Farrell, Louis Barreau, Alice Lebant, Valeria Famularo and Mathilde Lepage-Bagatta; Trinity Laban Conservatoire of Music and Dance, London. JAMES KEATES

they have no intentional relationship or purpose, other than speed and durational change. Thus there is no intentional emotional development or climax, which is why Cunningham's work is often referred to as abstract, although Merce Cunningham always refuted this, stating that it was people doing it, and people cannot be abstract.

> *Cunningham's dances celebrate the states of uncertainty and simultaneity that characterize modern life and art. They decentralize space, and telescope or stretch time, and allow for sudden unison activity, repetition, and rich variety and dispersal. They do away with the familiar comfort and predictability of dance movement that follows either a musical struc-ture, a story, a psychological make-up, or the demands of a proscenium stage-frame.*[86]

Cunningham also instigated a radical approach to choreography in the use of chance procedures. He would allow the decision for the structuring of his work – such as how many repetitions of certain phrases of movement, or where these phrases would be performed in the space, and how many dancers would do the phrase – to be left to the roll of a dice or turn of a card. As Banes states:

> *He may use chance methods like tossing coins or dice or picking cards to determine the order of movements in a phrase, sequence of phrases in a dance, places on stage to put the dancers, number of dancers to use in a section, or parts of the body to be activated. Chance subverts habits and allows for new combinations. It also under-mines literal meanings attached to sequences of movements or combinations of body parts.*

But Cunningham's program does not allow for improvization by the dancers or spontaneous determination of phrases, since the speed and complexity of his movements would make certain situations physically dangerous. Once determined, the paths and positions of the dancers must be exact.[87]

Randomness was then brought into the structure of the choreography, rather than the planning of linear development or narrative or expression. Phrases of material would be made without an expressive function beyond the human execution of the movement itself, and arranged by chance. 'Cunningham was not interested in making sure the audience "gets" a particular message from a dance, but rather in presenting a variety of experiences – aural, visual, kinetic – which the spectator is free to interpret or simply absorb.'[88]

THE TECHNIQUE

Cunningham used the technique he created as a method of preparing his dancers for the choreographic work he wanted to produce, as well as preparing the body in a systematic way with a 'physical logic'.[89] He devised the technique through his own body, and taught it to professional and semi-professional dancers. His focus on space, and the equal value of all directions, is visible in the technical movement language he created, in that the clarity of the body in space is very apparent. The motion of the body creates lines and curves which can occur in any direction and be produced by any part of the body with equal value.

The performance energy instigated by this approach to space is very distinct from the emotional force and projection of Graham Technique. In Cunningham Technique the energy is more

Fig. 66: Pliés. Cunningham class taught by Hannah Cameron, featuring dancers Alisha Stanley and Holly Smith; Trinity Laban Conservatoire of Music and Dance, London. JAMES KEATES

Fig. 67: Creating lines in Cunningham technique. Cunningham class taught by Gary Lambert, featuring dancers Alice Lebant and Valeria Famularo; Trinity Laban Conservatoire of Music and Dance, London. JAMES KEATES

contained within the three-dimensional sphere that constitutes the space around the body within the reach of the body – the kinesphere. Cunningham and his dancers disseminated the technique in their own teaching of other dancers as the work became increasingly popular and highly influential. Cunning- ham Technique has been taught in many professional dance training programmes as a named form. Teachers of the form utilize the technique as a methodology for teaching technical skills to student dancers, and not just as a way of accessing Cunningham's choreography.

In creating his technique Cunningham took elements from ballet technique and Graham Technique and combined them, creating something entirely different in the process. He combined the use of the torso from Graham Technique, with the intricacies of the foot and leg work of ballet technique. The Cunningham Technique class commences from an upright standing posture, emphasizing verticality, which is similar to ballet. Unlike Graham Technique, there is no floor work in Cunningham Technique; there is movement of the pelvis, but the pelvis is not a base of support in the technique, thus support through the legs, and balance of the centre of gravity in relation to the feet, is an essential focus.

There are structural elements of Cunningham Technique that evolved from ballet and Graham, such as some of the musical structures. For example, there are leg exercises done at different speeds and in rhythms similar to ballet, and exercises titled by the time structure, including an exercise with the same name as a Graham exercise, *exercise on 6*.

In Cunningham Technique the body has many centres of motion which facilitate articulation of different body parts. For example, the centre for the movement of the arm is the shoulder, and the centre of movement for the leg is the hip, and this emphasizes the articulation of the joints. The spine is identified as having different sections and different centres, which can be worked separately or together. Parallel and turned out legs are used in standing and gesturing.

In some of the patterns in the arm movements and leg gestures there are similarities to structures in ballet technique, and positions from ballet are used, such as first, second, fourth and fifth positions of the arms and feet, and attitude and retire positions for the legs. However, all of these can be done in parallel and turned out, creating far more possible variations and without details of the ballet aesthetic, such as épaulement (small rotations in the shoulders with frequent corresponding slight turn of the head) or a soft placement of the fingers. Cunningham said: 'The movements do have a certain emphasis on line, but the line is not at all a classical ballet line'.[90]

There are class structures that are similar to ballet (which were also incorporated into Graham Technique) such as *tendús* (extending the legs with the toes on the floor) and *pliés* (articulations of the leg joints when weight bearing). Cunningham also included musical aspects of the ballet class, such as *adagio* (slow sustained movement) and *allegro* (jumps) sections. There is a clear involvement of the spine in all aspects of the class, which is mobilized as much as the arms and legs. All aspects of the body have equal weight and purposefulness, and there is no hierarchy of movements. As Ellen Van Schuylenburch, a founder member of the Michael Clark Company and who studied at the Cunningham Studio, says: 'There is no value in a high jump, it is what it is. No hierarchy in a little hop; it is just as good as standing still; it is just as good as moving your hips.'[91]

THE BODY

Cunningham Technique works the torso as a limb, advocating precise articulation and shaping of the spine as much as the arms and legs. 'One of his technical advancements, related to ballet's five positions of the feet, he referred to as "five positions of the back: upright, curve, arch, twist and tilt".'[92] These actions of the spine are discussed below.

UPRIGHT

The upright action is the straight line of the torso in the upright position, or in hinges of the whole torso forward from the hips or backwards from the knees. The hinge action is created from the joints in the legs, and the relationship between the pelvis and spine is maintained. In forward hinges from the hips the weight should not shift backwards through the pelvis and sitting bones: the aim is to keep the pelvis above the feet as much as possible. (*See* Figure 70.)

CURVE

The curve action is forward flexion created from the lumber and thoracic spine, creating a long curve in the torso upwards and forwards from the pelvis. The placement of the pelvis is not changed, and the head follows the line of the curve. (*See* Figure 68.)

Fig. 68: Students working on the Cunningham curve. Cunningham class taught by Hannah Cameron, featuring dancers Jessica Chambers and Aisha Stanley; Trinity Laban Conservatoire of Music and Dance, London. JAMES KEATES

ARCH

The arch action is hyperextension of the upper spine created from the thoracic vertebrae, and lift upwards through the whole torso. The pelvis and lumbar spine remain upright. There is no forward shift in the ribs, or tilt in the pelvis. The back of the skull finishes slightly behind the back of the pelvis. (*See* Figure 69.)

TWIST

The twist action is the turning of the upper torso whilst maintaining the direction of the pelvis, creating torsion in the spine so that the front of the chest and shoulders face a different direction to the pelvis. The head and focus turn with the spine, generally achieving the same orientation as the chest and shoulder line. (*See* Figure 70.)

TILT

The tilt action is side flexion of the lumbar and thoracic spine, creating a long curve in the torso upwards and sideways (right or left) from the pelvis.

Fig. 69: Arch. Cunningham class taught by Hannah Cameron, featuring Holly Smith and Lewis Sharp; Trinity Laban Conservatoire of Music and Dance, London. JAMES KEATES

Fig. 70: Hinge and twist. Cunningham class taught by Hannah Cameron, featuring dancers Holly Smith and Lewis Sharp; Trinity Laban Conservatoire of Music and Dance, London. JAMES KEATES

The placement of the pelvis is not changed, and the head follows the line of the curve. (*See* Figure 71.)

As the technique uses the vertical standing position, spinal motion is facilitated by stability through clarity of the support of the centre of gravity through the legs and feet. At times the pelvis is an anchor for that stability, and provides a counterweight for the movement of the weight of the head in space through the actions of the spine. To access mobility in flexion of the lumbar spine the pelvis is sometimes tilted posteriorly (backwards) in particular exercises, and sometimes anteriorly (forwards) to take the straight torso off the vertical in hinges – but the relationship of the centre of gravity to the feet

Fig. 71: Students working on the Cunningham tilt. Cunningham class taught by Gary Lambert, featuring dancers Georgia Heighway and Lea Pointelin; Trinity Laban Conservatoire of Music and Dance, London.

Fig. 72: Trinity Laban students in Cunningham event re-staged by Daniel Squire. Trinity Laban BA2 Historical Projects 2015. Trinity Laban Conservatoire of Music and Dance, London. JAMES KEATES

needs to be understood. The lumbar and thoracic spine is utilized as fully as possible either in parts or as a whole. As Cunningham stated: 'All of the work comes from the trunk, from the waist, nearest the hip, and you tilt it or you twist it in every direction.'[93]

The head is carried with flexion and hyperextension of the spine (curves and arches) bringing it off the vertical, but the weight of the head is not released, and there is little flexion in the cervical spine. As Rachel Burn, a Cunningham teacher and choreographer who studied at the Cunningham Studio in New York, states: 'Your head is finishing off what has been set up in the body, rather than doing something extra.' However, the specificity in the spine in different exercises is very important, and there can be subtle distinctions. As Stephen Berkeley White, a Cunningham teacher and dancer for Diversions Dance Company (now National Dance Company Wales), Wayne McGregor's Random Dance and Mark Bruce Company, states:

There are many different types of back curve. You can perform an upper back curve, a middle back curve with the head up and the focus front, and a middle back curve with the head down as part of the curve; you can have a lower back curve that changes the position of the pelvis.[94]

So the class structure teaches precise articulation of the torso. The head is carried with the rotation of the torso in twists, so the direction of the eyes

Fig. 73: Shape and clarity. Cunningham class taught by Gary Lambert, featuring dancers Georgia Highway and Silvio Sighinolfi; Trinity Laban Conservatoire of Music and Dance, London. JAMES KEATES

Fig. 74: Leg extensions. Cunningham class taught by Hannah Cameron, featuring dancers Alisha Stanley and Jessica Chambers; Trinity Laban Conservatoire of Music and Dance, London. JAMES KEATES

relates to the facing of the shoulders and chest. The head is not used separately from the torso as a medium of expressive intent through spatial projection, or as a contrast to the motion in the torso such as in Graham spiral or pleadings.

The arms create lines and curves in space and move with the actions of the spine. The sensation is that the arms are clear and strong with the strength coming from the back, supported through the muscles in the back and the scapula (shoulder blades) (*see* Figure 73). The arms have a feeling of strength through precision and clarity. Unlike Graham, the arms in Cunningham Technique do not have an expressive function beyond the spatial form, although they could be said to frame the space in the upper kinesphere through the relationship to actions in the torso or legs.

The legs are then worked to achieve the same possibilities of line and curve as the arms within the spatial sphere of the lower body. The legs are bent or straight in either standing or gesturing movements, and require clarity and control. Cunningham said, '...

the arms are easy to move, so one doesn't know how to hold them, whereas the effort to move the legs makes you concentrate on how to move them.'[95]

Every movement of the limbs (including the spine) is performed with the accompanying clarity of the support of the body in standing. An understanding of grounding and strength in supporting from the floor – the feet, the legs and the centre of gravity – is part of every exercise. Balance is very important in the technique (you can hear Cunningham talking about balance in a short video on the website: https://www.mercecunningham.org/the-work/cunningham-technique/).

PRECISION, CLARITY AND DEFINITION

Precision, clarity and definition are key words to consider in the practice of this technique. Cunningham de-emphasized the organic bodily structures and passionate performance mode of the Graham style towards a form that is more cerebral in approach. The emphasis is on control and the thinking in the body. The movement patterns can become very complex, but the dancer should always appear active in the control of the movement, and in charge of the abstract puzzle of the complex forms. This thinking in the body should provide a physical weight and presence in the performance of the structures, as the awareness of finding balance and precision and inter-relationships in the body in the moment of doing the action is imperative.

As William Aitchison (Programme Leader for the BA Contemporary Dance Foundation Year programme at Trinity Laban) says, you need to figure out '...where is the energy coming from: is it coming from the floor in terms of stability into your centre to radiate out? Is it coming from the arms connecting into your back, which connects down into your centre?'[96] In this way the person doing the movement in *their* body is the dancing.

SPACE

Spatial structures are vital in this technique, as opening up the use of space and democratizing it from the frontal orientation of previous dance forms was

Fig. 75: Working with different fronts. Ellen Van Schuylenburch teaching a Cunningham class; Trinity Laban Conservatoire of Music and Dance, London. JAMES KEATES

a significant motivator of Cunningham's work. Ellen Van Schuylenburch says: 'Wherever I am facing is the front, any spot in space is as good as another.'[98] All surfaces of the body are equally energized, as there is no emphasis on frontal orientation or expression through the face. The performer does not project to the audience, but uses energy equally in three dimensions into all directions and from all surfaces. The consciousness of how you use space is embedded in the physicality and aesthetic (see Figure 72).

As there is no automatic reference to front, teachers sometimes create changing orientations in class sequences. For example, Rachel Burn says that '… negotiating space – having to be present to nego-

THE DANCER'S BODY

I think Merce Cunningham always allowed a person's body to be their body, and so there was never a need for an external aesthetic to be met. If this is where your second position is today that is OK, and if this is where your second position always is, that is right, that is completely right and your body is doing that. So if you have a whole company or a whole class doing the same sequence, it can look very different on each body.[97]

DANCING IN THREE DIMENSIONS

Stephen Berkeley-White says: You are three-dimensional beings in three-dimensional space; but the thing about watching everything flat is that it's like seeing things on a TV screen, and it doesn't actually have to be like that at all. In the same way that an audience doesn't have to sit on seats in front of you, they can be around you and amongst you. It's up to you to explore that.[99]

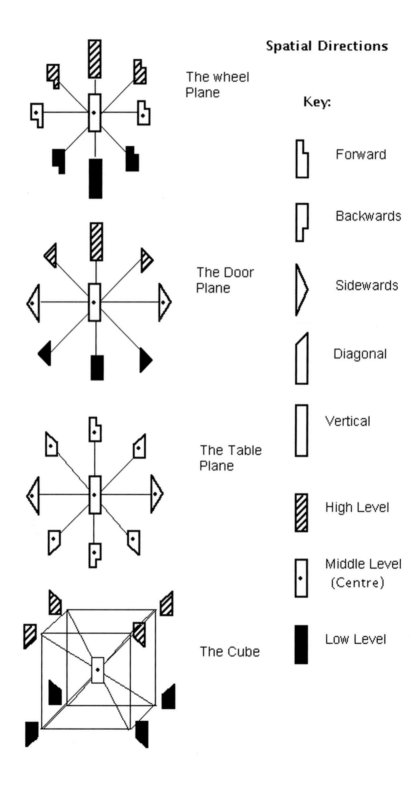

The wheel Plane

The Door Plane

The Table Plane

The Cube

Spatial Directions

Key:

Forward

Backwards

Sidewards

Diagonal

Vertical

High Level

Middle Level (Centre)

Low Level

Fig. 76: Diagram of twenty-seven spatial locations.

tiate' can be an important factor in engaging with the performance of the technique form, so she sets sequences in which the students all choose their own facing. This can lead to an active negotiation of space in the moment when their movement overlaps or legs cross. 'I really encourage them that if you meet someone's eyes or if your hands brush, then you can acknowledge that moment, keep going, don't let it distract you, but that thing really happened so don't pretend in didn't.' She then encourages an acknowledgment that: '…that is performing, that is being present, that is aliveness.'[100]

Movements lead the limbs to spatial locations in many dimensional directions, the three main dimensions being *sagittal* (forwards/backwards), *lateral* (left/right) and *vertical* (up to the ceiling/down to the floor). The sagittal and lateral directions each have three possibilities: *high, middle and low level*. For example, a forward direction for an arm can be on the level of its centre, that is, shoulder level (called 'middle level' in Labanotation); higher than

the shoulder ('high level' – 45 degrees above middle level); or lower than the shoulder ('low level' – 45 degrees below middle level). There are also *diagonals* (forward right diagonal/back left diagonal, forward left diagonal/ back right diagonal), which can also be high, middle or low. This makes twenty-seven possibilities of spatial location that have equal value in this form.

The curves or lines in the arms and legs can potentially be in any of these directions, with the distal end of the limbs – that is, the hands, feet or head – reaching these destinational points at the completion of each movement. The torso accesses high level locations through curves, tilts and arches, and middle level locations in hinges forwards from the hips. The torso accesses the diagonals through simultaneously twisting and curving forwards or arching backwards. Cunningham's use of diagonal locations, added to the complexity of the work in the spine in combining curve or arch simultaneously with twists, developing strength in the torso muscles.

Fig. 77: Diagonal directions achieved with the spine. Cunningham class taught by Hannah Cameron, featuring dancers Alisha Stanley and Jessica Chambers; Trinity Laban Conservatoire of Music and Dance, London. JAMES KEATES

Fig. 78: Moving into and out of 'body design'. Cunningham class taught by Gary Lambert, featuring dancer Phoebe Hart; Trinity Laban Conservatoire of Music and Dance, London. JAMES KEATES

The use of lines and curves in space can be manifested in three ways:

• in the sphere of space immediately around the body, known as the kinesphere
• in the general space being moved in (the studio or theatre)
• in the body itself, in terms of the shapes formed by the body

Cunningham Technique emphasizes the shaping in the body, called 'body design' in choreological practice.[101] Cunningham Technique utilizes a series of spatial forms in the body, either straight or curved, and the clarity of this shaping is important to the aesthetic. To create the dynamic qual-

ity of the spatial forms you need to feel the energy of the physical body creating shape, as well attention to the form in space: as Cunningham said: '… energy and shape: I try to bring them together as much as I can.'[102] An arm gesture is the creating of a spatial form in the body, a linear or curving shaping in space.

The intention to create spatial structure within the body then becomes the reason for the movement, rather than an unconscious product. The spatial form is actualized by the body, rather than there being an intention to create spatial energy beyond the body: there is no spatial projection (*see* Chapter 2) or spatial tension (energy in the space between two things).[103] The use of space is direct, in that the destination point of the movement is certain, and there is clarity and purposefulness in the approaching. This implies that there is no superfluous movement, and no hesitation or indulgence in the progress.

This does not imply that the movement is always fast or impactive – that is, hitting a finishing point through an increase of speed at the end of the movement.[104] Movement can be sustained, but there is a feeling of surety in the movement's purpose in space. Rachel Burn describes that in relation to her training in Cunningham: '…because it was so much about clarity I felt safe in thinking that whatever I am doing, I know what it should be.'[105] The clear emphasis is on the spatial form in the body, and the movement progresses into the design; however, it is not positional, in that the motion continues into and out of a location and into the next.

For dancers, finding clarity in the way into the destination is the work. Ellen Van Schuylenburch acknowledges that it is easy to 'want to fix everything to one spot…what I really emphasize – it's about movement, it is how you move from one to the next.'[106] Rachel Burn agrees, and states 'the journeying of the body is the dancing', and she adds: '…the aim isn't to be at point A and then to be at point B, it is to do that journey through point A and point B',[107] and to make that journey clear and clean and articulate.

ACTION

In Cunningham Technique the energy is held within the body, making the action of the body itself, rather than the emotion of the body, the most visible aspect of the performer. As Ellen Van Schuylenburch says: 'You don't express emotions, we don't express how we feel about the movement… the performative aspect is you in space, space and time and your body, you are the poetry of it, that is all it is.'[109] This performance mode is distinct from the passionate performance required by Graham in her technique, which is more ecstatic and emotional, projecting energy beyond the body.

Cunningham stated: 'I want it done clearly without anything about expression. So you see the

CUNNINGHAM 1952

'…what is seen, is what it is.'[108]

movement on that person, not something he or she adds…'[110] The act of doing the movement, the 'action content'[111] is the performative: the physical energy of engaging in the act of moving. In this way the action of the body in space and time becomes the primary focus. Daniel Squire, who danced in the Merce Cunningham Dance Company, quotes Cunningham in saying: 'When I dance, it means this is what I am doing.'[112] This action content is derived from the emphasis of the three dynamic factors: time, space and weight.[113]

The clarity of destination and the emphasis on achieving an intentional action creates a knowingness and self-possession in the Cunningham performance mode. The movement can become highly complex through changes in orientation and different destinations for different parts of the body. However, the fact that the destinations are established can make moving through them feel like solving a puzzle. Picking up and executing the quick-changing orientations and changing relationships between upper and lower body patterns can be satisfying, like completing a crossword or solving a riddle.

Stephen Berkeley White agrees: 'When things get very complicated people respond almost in a mathematical way to the logic of it and the problem solving of it.'[114] And Rachel Burn concurs: 'I always enjoyed in Cunningham the sort of mathematical equations of doing it: so you add this twist on to this curve and to this plié, and then you take away the curve…'[115]

What this process of learning can provide is the clarity of articulation in the body through the conscious voluntary control of the movement of the body, which becomes part of your technical ability.

Fig. 79: Bringing the elements together. Cunningham class taught by Hannah Cameron, featuring dancers Alisha Stanley and Jessica Chambers; Trinity Laban Conservatoire of Music and Dance, London. JAMES KEATES

However, Berkeley White highlights that you must not become too attached just to the mental challenge, and should stay physically responsive in the body. He states: 'Once you have got that, it is moving through space.'[116]

DYNAMICS

Cunningham Technique focuses on the dynamics of time, space and weight. Time as a dynamic property ranges through all possible sensorial feelings of time, from very fast (termed 'sudden' by Laban, as

extreme speed tends to be in short bursts) to very slow (termed 'sustained' by Laban[117], as very slow movement takes a duration of time to be visible).

To achieve the dynamic of time in movement performance the dancer must focus on and attend to the feeling in the body of the time structures of the movement. It is not sufficient to try and keep up with a musical beat or listen to accompaniment – rather, the dancer needs to produce the time structure so it is expressed by the body. Utilizing time is to make decisions and be decisive. Jowitt exclaims that 'Merce is dedicated to the image of a deci-

CUNNINGHAM 1985

If you emphasize activity, steps, a lot of movement, but the clarity of the positions is not very great, that isn't very satisfactory. Now, if you keep that energy in it, clarify the positions more at the same time, that is especially interesting. Ordinarily what happens is that one or the other begins to get lost. The basic thing about Dancing is the energy, and an amplification of it which comes through the rhythm, and if you lose that you end up in decoration.[119]

sion'.[118] The dancer decides to move into a direction, into a location, into a shape with a certain speed and duration. Thus the dancer, as decision maker, is in control.

When space and time qualities are engaged with together, a particular performance mode is reached. A mentally alive state, which Laban called 'awake',[120] is generated, which brings energy to the eyes and brain and a feeling for attention to the immediate external environment. This is a lively presence but a controlled one, enabling the performer to appear in control with a consciousness of the reality of the immediate environment. The thinking and mental energy is, however, in the bodily execution and not expressed in the face; as Daniel Squire says: '…you compute things whilst keeping a very even gaze.'[121]

The third motion factor is weight. In Cunningham Technique the use of the dynamic of weight is not about heaviness or releasing into gravity (as in Humphrey Limon Technique or Release-based Tech-

Fig. 80: Adagio. Cunningham class taught by Hannah Cameron, featuring dancers Jessica Chambers, Holly Smith and Alisha Stanley; Trinity Laban Conservatoire of Music and Dance, London. JAMES KEATES

Fig. 81: Creating a curve in space. Cunningham class taught by Gary Lambert, featuring dancer Silvio Sighinolfi; Trinity Laban Conservatoire of Music and Dance, London. JAMES KEATES

nique), nor its opposite in expressing lightness and suspending in space (as in the romantic ballet) – nor is it about expressing strength with bound flow as an emotional force (as in Graham). The weight factor in Cunningham is about the weight of the physical presence of the person.

The emphasis on time and space can lead to a cerebral approach to the execution of the technique – with the energy in the head. To balance this cognitively awake force the attention to the physical presence of the weight of the body in space and time is necessary. Jowitt emphasized this in describing the dancers in the Cunningham company as 'intensely alert to time and space – they are as self-possessed about their weight as animals'.[122] Attention to the

sensation of the body, and the feeling of the presence of the physical body in space and in time, is therefore an important performance consideration. All three factors need to be in play. At times, one or another may feel dominant, but maintaining all three can be the key. As Cunningham said:

Produce the rhythm; canalize the energy and sustain it; achieve the positions. It's like constantly trying to balance*, that's what can be lively in it. Taken alone, none of the three is sufficient.*[123]

Although Cunningham's choreography has no expressive intention in terms of communicating anything outside the dancers' movement, dancers can still feel the expression of themselves in it, as they are it. The expression of time and space and weight in the physical presence of doing, is an intentional act. As Stephen Berkeley White says: 'You use the form of what you're given to express through it.'[124] This expression is the physical sensation of the effort in the action: the feeling of motion in the spine and in the musculature of the abdomen and back.

Generating this sensorial dimension leads to a fullness in the use of the body, as every curve can deepen, every twist, twist more. Maintaining the work in the moment of doing means the energy is not about making a fixed shape, but physically fulfilling the action to the developing edge of your ability.

RELATIONSHIPS

In Cunningham Technique all combinations of events in different parts of the body are theoretically possible. Curves in the torso can be accompanied by curves or lines in the arms and legs in any direction within the range of the body. There is no intentional meaning behind the combinations in any moment – there are simply co-existent constituents of the overall form. This is exemplified by the class practice, as the preparatory work is separated into short specific exercises for different parts of the body. Body areas are worked separately, promoting articulation of the joints, and then the elements are brought together in combination.

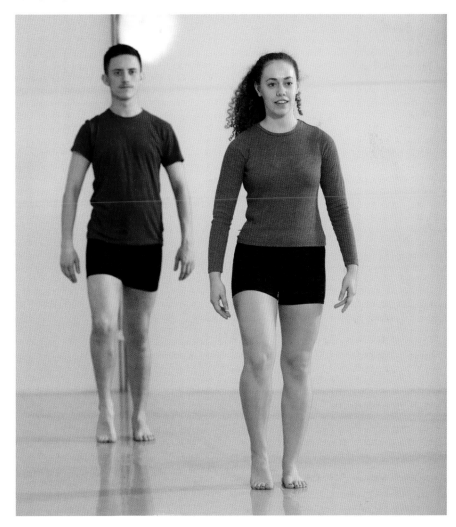

Fig. 82: Articulating the feet. Cunningham class taught by Hannah Cameron, featuring dancers Holly Smith and Lewis Sharp; Trinity Laban Conservatoire of Music and Dance, London. JAMES KEATES

Fig. 83: Lines and curves. Cunningham class taught by Gary Lambert, featuring dancers Georgia Heighway and Silvio Sighinolfi; Trinity Laban Conservatoire of Music and Dance, London. JAMES KEATES

Sequences (such as adagio, triplets and travelling jumps) combine the possibilities engaged with in the start of class, in combinations that include motion of the arms, torso and legs with changes in orientation. These combinations create challenging structures of inter-relationships through the complexity of dealing with simultaneous structures in the body. So the combinations support an active mind in that,

as Ellen Van Schuylenburch states: 'You have to be alert, you have to pick up.'[126]

Elements are not integrated to make a whole expression – rather, one movement can exist at the same time as another, or not. Of course when moving, the body is an integrated whole and so in the dancer the elements come together seamlessly – but each still needs full completion and balanced physical intention,

CUNNINGHAM 1985

With the aim of 'the legs and back working together, we alternate: legs firmly held, we work on the back, then we come to the legs, and in order to isolate them, I keep the back still and do leg exercises. After that we put the legs and back together.'[12]

energy and emphasis: for example, the arms should not be dominant and the torso passive. This is true within Cunningham's choreography in that:

...there are often implied situations and relationships in the dances the company does, but none that has a dramatic impact. Incidents aren't stressed: the dancers don't use that kind of timing. One is entertained solely by the formal values of dancing – by what Cunningham...described as 'the passage of movement from moment to moment in a length of time'.[127]

The technical skill is then in producing the clean efficiency in creating and moving between the elements. This requires clarity of articulation in the joints, and a clear understanding of how to support and balance the body in gravity. The aim is to have nothing superfluous to the clarity of these elements. There is no affectation, no flourishes, and yet each individual has to find themselves within the structures so that they bring them to life through their execution. This is very distinct from imposing structures on your body – rather, the structures are actualized through your body. Rachel Burn says:

Students sometimes think that the external thing is the result – is what they are aiming

for – but...you work in what your body does, and you obviously push the limits of it, but you respect your body and know what your body is. There is nothing external governing that.[128]

Stephen Berkeley-White says:

Use it to organize your body; use it to become strong.[129]

MUSIC AND SOUND

Rhythm and speed of motion is important in this technique. Cunningham classes incorporate exercises with very distinct time structures, similar to the practices within a ballet class and a Graham class where different exercises have a certain time signature, a pace and use of rhythm. Exercises are usually counted, and there is usually a musical accompaniment that corresponds to the metric structures of the exercises (unlike in Cunningham's choreography). The music then supports the clarity of the pulse and rhythm of the movements.

Counting numbers is not essential in working with rhythm, pulse and speed changes, but it can be a way of the teacher communicating and the dancers discovering rhythmic patterns in the body. Stephen

CUNNINGHAM 1952

Now time can be an awful lot of bother with the pinch-penny counting that has to go on with it, but if one can think of the structure as a space of time in which anything can happen in any sequence of movement event, and any length of stillness can take place, then the counting is an aid towards freedom, rather than a discipline towards mechanization.[130]

Berkeley White states:

> Just because you are used to [the teacher] counting this out doesn't mean that you have to do that in your own brain, but you do have to be rhythmical. So you have to find your own rhythm; if there is music in the room you have to attach to that rhythm, if there is no music in the room you have to find that in yourself.[131]

Rachel Burn supports that in stating that there is a 'balance between something being specific, and you need to meet that specificity, and balancing that with what you need to do in order to get there.' She states that this is particularly true when it comes to timings; when you need to accomplish an action within a specified time frame, or perform a sequence of actions but arrive on a specific beat, each individual needs to work out how to meet that requirement in their personal execution. She says: 'There is more than one way of doing something.'[132]

The exercise *back stretches* is sustained and continuous, which means that the pace is slow and the movement is smooth, with no rhythmic accents. Foot exercises tend to have clear rhythmic structures, often subdividing beats with quite a quick pace. There is often an *adagio* exercise, which requires controlled use of time to move at a slow pace. That pace can be very slow: Ellen Van Schuylenburch talks about 'keeping time, which is really difficult at the beginning... slow is very slow. It really is 1, then you lift your leg on 2, you hold on 3,

Fig. 84: Cunningham class being taught by Ellen Van Schuylenburch; Trinity Laban Conservatoire of Music and Dance, London. JAMES KEATES

maybe you tilt on 4, 5, slowly, 6, 7...' The movement in classes also takes you through 'sequences that are very fast, very slow and very complex'.[133]

Feeling these time distinctions, and attending to the expression of visible time structures that you are creating with the movement, will not only generate the quality of performance, but also support the technical execution of the material.

STRUCTURES OF A CUNNINGHAM CLASS

Cunningham Technique is known as a codified technique in that it has a clear set of parameters and structures and includes set exercises. However, this does not mean that it is rigid and immovable. Cunningham had no desire for his technique class to be a completely set structure even though the aesthetic is very clear. The class structure supports a systematic preparation of the body in a series of exercises that work each part of the body and then bring them together, as well as exploring a range and variety of rhythmic structures met through those exercises.

Daniel Squire concurs, stating that Merce 'always wanted the technique to remain fluid'.[134] This again correlates to his choreographic practice in that 'Cunningham, having created extraordinary dancing, then goes as far as he can to make it feel risky, to keep himself and the dancers from ever fixing it down, from feeling complacent.'[135] He would often challenge his dancers by creating performances known as 'Events', in which sections of choreography from other works would be re-used in different orders with a new set of scenographic elements (costumes, set, décor) and a new musical score.

This process further exemplified the idea that the movement had no intentional meaning and could be re-structured, re-ordered and re-combined. Moreover, the Events exemplified the co-existence of theatrical elements, purposefully subverting any integration through the acknowledgment of the re-combination.

The longevity of Cunningham's career meant that his work, his working process and his technique

Fig. 85: Backwards hinge and twist. Cunningham class taught by Hannah Cameron, featuring dancer Lewis Sharp; Trinity Laban Conservatoire of Music and Dance, London. JAMES KEATES

have become very established practices, but also that they have changed and developed over time. The classical Cunningham class has a structure, and there are some sequences that have become established and 'set'. Other exercises have a specific body use, such as the attention on a particular part of the body, but the content is designed to change, meaning there are new combinations made all the time. This supports active thinking and movement memory. 'My point was to make people strong and resilient in the head rather than giving the same class every day, to give them some kind of elasticity about technique.'[136]

CUNNINGHAM 1985

'...in every class, and after the warming up exercises which should take a good deal of time, at some moment the student should touch the utmost limits of what he is capable of, then, and every day, he should achieve that and enlarge it.'[137]

There is a structure to the classes, but within that there are also endless possibilities for variation of the elements. Daniel Squire states:

There is an exercise called the 'exercise on 6' which is a 'set exercise' – there are different ways of teaching it, and there are different things that happen to the pelvis; some people teach that at one point you are in an arch or a hinge, and other people teach that you are in a hinge but no arch, while other people teach that you are in a plié but not a hinge and an arch on that particular count.[138]

Moreover, each Cunningham class is taught in a context, and often separate from training dancers to perform Cunningham choreography. Ellen Van Schuylenburch states that 'there is definitely a structural core'.[139] Each teacher will use the structures and elements of a class distinctly according to how they have inherited knowledge of the technique, how they use that within the situation they are teaching in, and also in relation to the students they are working with. Daniel Squire says that his approach:

...varies on the particular situation whether I would teach it as I have seen it taught in

New York, and if so whether I have seen it taught by Merce or people who were given a lot of responsibility in the company or in the [Cunningham] Foundation, or whether it was by some of the other teachers who were further from that. I use a mixture of those things, and sometimes I come up with a new way and sometimes I use someone else's way, and that can vary, dependent on what I am seeing.[140]

Furthermore, every student new to Cunningham has to start learning the practice of the technique, and building the skills to be able to do the technique in all of its potential complexity. When new to the technique the teacher might go quite slowly to support learning of the fundamental structures. Once these structures are known, then the practice in class can move quickly from one exercise to the next, so the students can find themselves within those structures and prepare their body to move through them. Stephen Berkeley White states 'there are a lot of short, structured exercises, they don't tend to go on forever. You constantly move on to the next thing.' He continues: 'Because it has structures, you can conceptualize it and relate that conceptualization to your understanding of the sensation of it.'[141]

The relationship of self to the movement structures has to be found by each dancer for themselves; William Aitchison says that students need:

...to find their own way of moving through material, their own way of performing that material, even though it is set within a framework...you watch what other people are doing, and if you see someone trying to do something within the material, then you can try and do that. And when you do it, you will do it in a different way to them, and then someone might see you do it and take on what you have done.[142]

To start the class, dancers should be present within the feeling of their physicality as well as present to the space around them. Rachel Burn states:

Fig. 86: Moving through general space. Cunningham class taught by Ellen Van Schuylenburch, featuring dancers Murielle Werthauer, Stephanie D'Arcy Collins, Eleni Stephanou, Vincenzo D'Acquisto, Jon Werede Hope, Jiaxin Yuan, Flora Grant and others. Trinity Laban Conservatoire of Music and Dance, London. JAMES KEATES

Before we start the bounces, I set the class up to lift the arches of the feet, lift their inner knee, lift their inner thigh and lower abdominals, release the back of the pelvis, release the front of the ribs and the sternum, let the shoulder blades rest, and then draw the spine up from the pelvis through the top of the head and let the shoulders hang broadly and then we start the bounces. For me that brings my weight upwards and slightly forwards over the balls of my feet.[143]

The Merce Cunningham Trust has made video documentaries of the Merce Cunningham Dance Company doing class, which are available to view on the internet called *Mondays with Merce* (Merce Cunningham Trust, 2013, 2016b, 2016a). These show Cunningham classes taught by Robert Swinston. The structures that you can see in these classes are described below.

BOUNCES

Class starts with flexion of the spine in different spatial directions. The spine creates a long curve from pelvis to skull, rather than a full flexion of every vertebrae. In the *bounces* 'your head is finishing off what has been set up in the body, rather than doing something extra.'[144] At first you curve and then gently pulse. The exercise is called 'easy bounces', but bouncing as such is not the action. The bounce, or pulsing, is generated through a small motion of the spine to create a slight increase and decrease in the depth of the spinal curve. This motion is to feel an opening and deepening of the curve, and exploration of the elasticity and flexibility within the structures of the body, and how large that curve could be in space.

BACK STRETCHES

In *back stretches* a sustained forward curve becomes a lengthening of the torso horizontal to the floor through the pelvis tipping forwards, and then the pelvis and spine return to the vertical in one piece. This is done in different standing positions; one iteration includes a twist before the curve, and then the lengthening happens towards a forward diagonal direction.

BACK CURVE

This action explores combinations of curve, twist and arch, upright whilst stationary in the feet.

THROUGH THE FOOT

This action involves articulating the feet and working the joints in the feet and ankles through pressing off the floor.

ARMS

Articulating the shoulder girdle: shoulder joint, shoulder blade, collar bones and moving the arms in space whilst maintaining a strong balanced support in the lower body.

EXERCISE ON 6

This exercise involves six bars of a given time signature, which can vary. It has a short pattern, but it is repeated with variations. It explores changes in the spine and pelvis whilst the feet are stationary. It can include twists, curves and arches, as well as hinges forwards and hinges backwards, creating a line upwards and backwards from the knees to the head. The emphasis is on full movement of the spine without losing stability.

ONE ARM OVER THE HEAD

This exercise is a spinal movement with the accompaniment of one arm gesturing.

EXERCISE ON 8, OR TWO ARMS OVER THE HEAD

This exercise consists of eight movements on eight

Fig. 87: Articulating the shoulder joint. Cunningham class taught by Hannah Cameron, featuring dancers Alisha Stanley and Jessica Chambers, Trinity Laban Conservatoire of Music and Dance, London. JAMES KEATES

counts. It integrates a fuller movement of both the arms with the use of the spine. The eight movements can look like simple shapes but they are hard to do, and variations can add difficulty, such as a rise on to the balls of the feet and the effect of that on trying to balance, or the addition of a lean backwards.

PLIÉS

Pliés are movements in the legs when supporting on two feet equally. The angles in the ankle, knee and hip joints change to allow the pelvis to move towards and away from the feet. *Demi (half) pliés* bring the pelvis down without the heels leaving the floor, and are done first; then *full pliés* are done, in which the heels are released from the floor in order to go lower (*see* Figure 66). Pliés can utilize the turned-out foot positions: first, heels together; second, feet apart; third, to left and right side; fourth, feet apart, one forward one back; and fifth, one foot crossed in front of the other. Pliés can be combined with tilts, twists, arches and curves of the spine, and curved or straight arms.

FOOT EXERCISES AND BRUSHES

These exercises articulate the feet and extend the legs with the toes generally not leaving the floor, or just leaving the floor. There can be several different versions of these exercises, which can incorporate shifts of weight from standing leg to gesturing leg, creating motion of the body off the spot. There can be a literal brushing of the feet on the floor, in sliding the foot out, from and back into standing. There can be the inclusion of a *pas de cheval* (step of the horse), borrowed from ballet vocabulary, which is a successional movement of the leg unfolding into a direction.

Gesturing of the legs can lead to weight transference on to two feet in different directions, and then a pushing off and returning to support on one leg – thus there is a testing of the balance after motion of the centre of gravity. There can be a leg exercise which is often a faster pace and includes different rhythms, including half and quarter notes that divide the beat. There are actions called beats, where one foot taps along the supporting leg in fast-paced rhythms.

Arm gestures are often used, and spinal motion can be added. Exercises are often done in parallel, then in turned out forwards, sideways and backwards with arm positions for each direction.

LEG EXTENSIONS

These are extensions of the legs in spatial directions with the foot extending off the floor. *Leg extensions* often also work in parallel forwards and then turned out forwards, sideways and backwards. There are many possible elements used in different exercises or combinations. Exercises can use circles of the legs from the hip both with the toe on the floor and with the leg lifted, finding clarity of articulation in the hip socket whilst balancing on one leg. High extensions of the whole leg are done with a throwing action without holding the leg in the air, and also slowly suspending the support of the leg in the air.

ADAGIO

This action involves slow and controlled movement involving leg extensions and balancing on one leg; it is often done with torso actions and accompanying arm gestures (*see* Figure 80).

TRIPLETS

Triplet is a travelling step. The origins of the Cunningham triplet are in Graham Technique. As described in Chapter 3, a triplet is a travelling movement that involves three steps, most often one at a low level (with a bend in the knees or plié), and two steps at high level (on the ball of the foot with the heels lifted/demi pointe). In Graham Technique these travel forwards, and turning can be added.

In Cunningham Technique the pattern of three steps can have many variations: there can be two low-level and one high-level step for example, and the steps can work in more directions – forwards, backwards and sideways, and each step in the sequence of three could be in any direction; the rhythm of the steps does not always have to be even. Some triplet steps in Cunningham can be under the centre of gravity and thus on the spot. Travelling steps in triplets are large, which takes conscious effort to achieve.

Many aspects of dance techniques challenge dancers to move in inorganic ways. These challenges require conscious control, and through that enable a growing awareness of the body. Daniel Squires provides an example:

Normally, most people if they were to walk backwards would take smaller steps than if they were to walk forwards. Fabulous. Are your legs shorter than they were? No. Are you less used to it? Yes. Does your pelvis operate differently? Yes. Is your relationship to gravity

Fig. 88: Triplet. Cunningham class taught by Hannah Cameron, featuring dancers Lewis Sharp and Holly Smith; Trinity Laban Conservatoire of Music and Dance, London. JAMES KEATES

because of all of that slightly different? Yes. All of the above. Can you take the steps just as large as you go backwards? Yes, but you need to pay attention differently to what you are doing.[145]

Whereas in Graham triplets the weight shifts from foot to foot with the back foot pushing off to shift the pelvis and propel the body forward into space, the Cunningham triplet situates weight on both feet for moments within the locomotion. This creates a greater stability through the legs and pelvis during the travelling, which allows for the addition of tilts, curves and arches in the spine without loss of balance. The motion of the spine most usually happens on the first low-level step of each triplet pattern, the torso then returning to an upright posture for the second step; however, as stated previously, any combination is possible. Each arch, tilt or curve of the spine has an accompanying arm movement.

The stability afforded by the weight being supported on two feet during the triplet also allows for fast changes in orientation. This creates far more spatial possibilities for the triplet, allowing the motion to shift in any direction and the dancer to be viewed from any side. The turns are barely visible between any of the three steps. The turn itself is not emphasized, so attention is given to the new facing achieved, and thus the change in orientation in general space. Triplet sequences can incorporate any other movement actions in combination.

JUMPS IN CENTRE

Jumps in Cunningham utilize all five types of elevation, as specified in the previous chapter:

* 1:1 – one foot to the same foot (*hop*)
* 1:2 – one foot to two feet (*assemble*)
* 2:2 – two feet to two feet (*jump*)

Fig. 89: Jumps. Cunningham class taught by Hannah Cameron, featuring dancers Alisha Stanley and Holly Smith; Trinity Laban Conservatoire of Music and Dance, London. JAMES KEATES

* 2:1 – two feet to one foot (*sissonne*)
* 1:1 – one foot to the other foot (*leap*)

As with other aspects of the technique, these can be done in turn out or in parallel, or from turn out to parallel, or vice versa. Jumps can also be done with the addition of turns to change orientation. Within a class, to facilitate bodily execution and reduce risk of injury, jumps will start with simple structures and then become more complex, and then more integrated with other movement material.

TRAVELLING JUMP

Travelling jumps can be combined with arm and leg and torso actions, and sequenced with other steps from the technique, such as triplets and balances, so the rhythmic structure of the whole often dictates the speed and thus the height of the jump. Within the array of structuring possibilities that allow for any combination of movements, a jump could end in a balance, another jump, a triplet or a standing pause, and be the beginning or end of a phrase.

CODIFIED TECHNICAL PRACTICE

There is a structure to the class that teachers either follow or use as a basis. Stephen Berkeley White says: 'There is a structure, so there is a sense of continuity. You know what that is, and you can come back to it again and again. There is a pattern that you understand, so there is a consistency in that.'146 Teachers using a Cunningham Technique approach can follow a classic structure for the classes they teach, but also may create a more hybrid approach in terms of combining exercises or adding other movement factors. William Aitchison says:

> I am quite interested in…having moments where the dancers can be free and move through the space and be less strict in terms of maybe counts and body positions and then have moments where everything is very clear and crisp. So trying to get both of those things in.147

So, Cunningham Technique can be a basis for contemporary technique classes as well as a more codified structured approach. Whatever the approach adopted by the teacher, there is a structural core to the practice, which not only supports the gaining of skills such as strength, articulation and balance, but also the possibility to experience yourself in relation to a particular set of movement and performance choices. As Daniel Squire says: 'Technique leads to more things being possible.'148

CHAPTER 5

RELEASE-BASED TECHNIQUE

BACKGROUND AND PRINCIPLES

Release, or Release-based Dance Technique as it is sometimes called in the UK, is an approach to teaching and learning in dance that was initiated in the USA by dancers seeking a new and different understanding and approach to the moving body. In the post-modernist movement in the 1960s and 1970s choreographers sought to forge new ways of presenting dance to an audience and new processes of creation. This led to dancers moving away from the idea of the 'superhuman' performer towards the reality of the person as a moving body, which challenged methods of training in dance and established techniques.[149] Artists such as Trisha Brown, Yvonne Rainer and Steve Paxton (who created Contact Improvisation) started to challenge assumptions about what movement could be considered as dance, and how dance movement could be sourced in the body.

With this idea, dancers explored other approaches to learning about, and through, bodily movement, and started to explore martial arts and somatic practices. The word somatic was coined by Thomas Hanna in 1976[150] and comes from the word 'soma', which refers to a person as an embodied self-regulating being, as distinct from viewing a body from a third-person perspective, or as a machine that is directed by the mind. Mary Ann Foster understands the term 'soma' as referring to 'the conscious, aware, awake body, the living, breathing, moving and thinking body'.[151] Somatic practices are ways for the experience of being an integrated body and mind, or, being an embodied person, to support self-awareness. Self-awareness through embodiment is used as a basis to support ease of motion and clarity of function in the body.

The sensory awareness of a person (how we perceive ourselves through our internal sense systems) and the motor function of an individual (how we move ourselves and control movement) are inextricably connected, which means that until you can perceive an aspect of your body and sense the function of it, you cannot control the motor function.[152] For those who engage in somatic practices, perception of bodily function is supported by providing physical sensorial experiences that enable the person to become aware, or more aware, of themselves as embodied beings. Often the practice involves actively finding a calm state to quieten the mind to enable greater clarity of sensorial perception when movement happens. Improved sensorial perception – also known as *kinaesthetic* awareness – can then improve motor function and control.

In somatic practices the embodied person is viewed as a holistic integrated system continually affected by internal and external factors, including their emotions, beliefs, behaviours and life experiences. As Thomas Hanna says: 'Somatic is a field of study dealing with somatic phenomena: that is, the human being as experienced by himself from the inside.'[153]

Dancers started to explore different practices instigated by influential thinkers/practitioners such as F. Matthias Alexander (who established the Alexander Technique), Moshe Feldenkrais (who established the Feldenkrais Technique), Mabel E. Todd (who established Ideokinesis). New somatic movement processes then emerged, such as Joan Skinner's Skinner Releasing, Bonnie Bainbridge

Fig. 90: Individual processes. Release class taught by Zoi Dimitriou, featuring dancers Lea Pointelin, Samantha Furnival and Giovanna Piccolo; Trinity Laban Conservatoire of Music and Dance, London. JAMES KEATES

Cohen's Body-Mind Centering, and Susan Klein's Klein Technique.

These practices were catalysts for dialogue about teaching dance and dance technique, which influenced many practitioners to explore new sets of teaching principles.[154] Joan Skinner coined the term 'Releasing' in relation to her own practice which became known as 'Skinner Releasing' when release as a term was adopted by various practitioners for different somatic-related dance and movement practices and approaches to technical training.

The somatic influence on dance practice then spread to the UK, and the influence of this approach became a key feature of a new wave of post-modernist choreographers in the UK, in what was termed 'New Dance'. Rosemary Butcher, the New Dance Collective and Siobhan Davies were artists associated with New Dance in the UK, and the dancers they worked with also became very influential in sharing and disseminating this approach through professional classes and then into dance training institutions.

A NEW APPROACH

Release-based Technique is distinct in its development from the other techniques described in this book, as this technique form has evolved from different influences, by many different dance practitioners, and thus has no clear direct lineage from any particular practitioner or practice. In this way it is not so easy to quantify it as a singular thing. It was not created as a training for a specific choreographic style, so learning processes are more open-ended. The approaches adopted exemplify an understanding of how movement is embodied and how movement skill can be learnt, and so can be seen as a pedagogical approach rather than as a form of technique. However, the title has been adopted within training institutions and practitioners as an umbrella title.

These so-named dance classes use a somatic approach, and use a movement practice to promote sensorial perception. Teachers of Release-based Technique utilize their individual knowledge of somatic practices and approaches to develop

Fig. 91: Release class taught by Zoi Dimitriou, featuring dancer Tiffany Desplanques; Trinity Laban Conservatoire of Music and Dance, London. JAMES KEATES

classes through their own subjective experiences, embodied knowledge and creativity. Individual dance teachers are influenced by different somatic practices, and also by different release-based dance teachers. Each individual teacher uses movement material of their own devising, which means there is no established conformity in the material used in this technique. The movement used can change from class to class and from teacher to teacher, or even from class to class with the same teacher. Students have to adapt, shift focus, and work with different elements.

Students are encouraged to assimilate new movement experiences into their possibilities for individual choices for movement, and are encouraged to explore the movement within their current range and ability so that there is no idealized form to aim for. This variation can support versatility through exploring approaches to moving, rather than a discreet set of skills, and in this way the technique can support an open-ended creative practice.

THE TECHNIQUE

Release-based Technique works from the premise that a person is an integrated body and mind as 'Somatic practices encourage a holistic experience of the self, integrating the mind and body, towards the concept of an actively 'lived' body'.[155] Internal perception of the self in motion, which can be known as the *kinaesthetic* experience, involves using information from the internal sense systems (proprioception and interoception). *Proprioception* can be defined as the ability to perceive the position and movement of our body from internal sensory information. *Interoception* can be defined as the information that comes to the brain about the condition of the body.[156] This is an important aspect of all dance techniques when not relying constantly on a mirror to check your external form.

Fig. 92: Moving on the floor. Release class taught by Melanie Clarke, featuring dancer Luca Braccia; Trinity Laban Conservatoire of Music and Dance, London. JAMES KEATES

However, the emphasis of the Release approach is to be explicit about using the proprioceptive and interoceptive experience as a precursor to creating movements in your own body. Rather than thinking of movement as something that brain initiates and then using proprioception to sense the results of that, in Release Technique you use awareness of sensation to perceive internally before and during the activation of movement. This is distinct from using imagery in the mind to activate a movement response, as Bonnie Bainbridge Cohen describes in her explanation of the work somatization:

> I use the word 'somatization' to engage the kinaesthetic experience directly, in contrast to 'visualization', which utilizes imagery to evoke a kinaesthetic experience. Through somatization the body cells are informing the brain as well as the brain informing the cells....When the body is experienced from within, the body and mind are not separated but are experienced as a whole.[157]

Somatic practices work with the premise of promoting individuals' perception of themselves as embodied beings through sensorial feedback. Thomas Hanna puts this clearly:

> It is a wonderful neurological fact that increasing bodily awareness means increasing neurological sensory awareness, and that this sensory awareness of the muscles goes hand in hand with voluntary motor control of the muscles. This is because the sensory-motor system is a 'feedback loop': in other words, if you cannot sense it, you cannot move it, and the more you can move it, the more you will sense it. This is a rule of the sensory-motor system, one solid part of the neurophysiological foundation of somatic education.[158]

This somatics is then related to our perception of ourselves through how we move and act in our environment. Perception of movement is a unification of all the sensorial information that can arise in the act of moving. Perception is a unified experience, and not a series of distinct sensations. In a simplistic example, we know smell is a constituent part of taste and the look of food influences our reaction to it – you artificially change the colour of a food, then people might have an immediate aversion to it; show someone from the UK a tasty insect and they might not want to try it. Perceptual channels integrate with and are relational with the entirety of our lived experience, our understanding that comes from being a person in the world. The somatic approach is about acknowledging this unification.

Thus you cannot separate the experience of now, to the experience of before, and the expectation of the future, so everything is dealt with in what can be termed the historical present. Somatic practices identify that experiences leave residue in the embodiment of people: you hold your past in how you hold your body. You cannot separate the person from their knowledge and experience, or the acquisition of new knowledge from a relationship to past knowledge. There is no blank slate.

CREATING AWARENESS THROUGH ATTENTION

The Release-based Technique approach aims to promote embodied awareness, then use that awareness to create greater specificity of choice in motion. The development of awareness is supported through attention training: you are requested to attend to your subjective experience. As we are complex organisms we could be overloaded with information on a constant basis, and we have a limited capacity of what we can take in.

Thus we learn to focus our attention, and we do this by shutting out the information that we don't want to deal with. We can attune our attention to the television programme we want to see, and tune out the perception of our body, which is slumped on the total support of our large sofa. Or, we attune to the text message we have just received, and have no awareness that we have stopped walking and are blocking the pavement for other pedestrians. These are processes of attuning attention outside the body.

Somatic practice uses this ability to attune, but brings it directly into the experience of the sensations

Fig. 93: Improvisation with a partner. Release class taught by Melanie Clarke, featuring Melanie Clarke, Luca Braccia, Rebecca Hunt, Holly Smith, Yu-Tzu Lin and Lewis Sharp; Trinity Laban Conservatoire of Music and Dance, London. JAMES KEATES

of our body perception. Perception of the body can be highly complex as it has so many layers. Also, everything we know and do with our body is in relation to the environment of the world around us, which brings with it our previously held knowledge and experience, our habits, our feelings and our relationship to what is going on around us. As Bonnie Bainbridge Cohen says in *An Introduction to Body-Mind Centering*:

It is through our senses that we receive information from our internal environment (ourselves) and the external environment (others and the world). How we filter, modify, distort, accept, reject and use that information is part of the act of perceiving.

When we choose to absorb information, we bond to that aspect of our environment. When we block out information, we defend against that aspect. Learning is the process by which we vary our responses to information based on the context of each situation.

In order to perceive clearly, our attention, concentration, motivation or desire must actively focus on what it is we are to perceive.[159]

So to develop awareness, teachers generate a calm and non-judgemental space, with time allocated for focusing in on the body. Classes are then structured to use a specificity of attention that clarifies the attunement, or what in Body-Mind Centering is called 'active focusing'[160] to specific aspects of the experience of moving.

Through that clarity of experience and the time allocated to it, individuals find an organization for their perception and can make meaning out of their kinaesthetic experience. Attention to the experience of moving can then create self-awareness through the person's own ability to perceive themselves in motion.

REFINEMENT FIRST

Release Technique works from a very different strategy from traditional dance technique practices, as the aim is to achieve refinement of movement straightaway. Traditionally it is thought that a dancer must first acquire gross motor skills (big actions using big muscle groups), then over time refine these to find more detail and fine motor skills (small actions with deeper muscle groups), and after that develop their creativity. Release works from the idea that you can first work with a refinement and more open creative exploration through very specific attention and focus, and then apply that to movement.

The clarity of intention in activating a movement is sought first. This means that the movement language is initially reduced in complexity, in layering or in the demand for acute movement memory, so that clarity can be worked on. You could spend time in a class focusing on how the head balances and moves on top of the spine using tiny movements with no set sequence or counts, no larger movements in space, no shift of weight, and no requirement to perform or interact with the environment.

This process develops a subtle awareness that can then be applied to larger movement of the spine, facilitating a freedom and mobility because there is no holding in the neck and skull. The ability to attend very specifically to the sensation of the freedom in movement of the skull, without focus on counts or

TRY THIS

Perhaps you can try making some very tiny movements with your skull without any movement of the neck. Find an easy sitting or standing position. Place your hands lightly around your neck to feel that it is still. Then, with your eyes closed or open, tilt the skull side to side or forwards and back with tiny movements. Turn the skull a little to the right and a little to the left. You can then try some small circles, still not moving the neck. Then start to draw a figure-eight with the top of the skull, and now let the rest of the spine join in. Through this activity you can develop the following:

- a subtle felt awareness for the skull on top of the spine
- use the feeling of how the balance receptors in the ears feel the changes in the skull's relationship to gravity
- explore how much mobility there is at the top of the spine
- learn how the head can move off vertical, and balance be maintained in standing and supporting the bodyweight (that is, you learn that moving the head does not mean that you fall over)
- become aware of how mobilizing the head can free the mobility of the spine

muscular activity or locomotion, and other aspects of the multi-layered complexity that is dance, is very different from stretching the large muscles of the neck whilst counting beats in music and adding an arm gesture. So the process enables an awareness that could very easily be missed completely without the possibility to focus deeply.

Fig. 94: Somatic hands-on practice. Release class taught by Melanie Clarke, featuring dancers Holly Smith and Rebecca Hunt; Trinity Laban Conservatoire of Music and Dance, London. JAMES KEATES

What this practice means is that not all of the time in the technique class is spent trying to find clarity of movement in space and time – rather, the focusing of attention is done through simple pared-down movement structures to develop the dancer's awareness. After this, the awareness gained can be applied to dance motion with increasing levels of complexity.

These pared-down movement forms are derived from different sources from different somatic practices to attend to perception and explore movement possibilities. Henry Montes (Release teacher and dancer with the Siobhan Davies Dance Company, Rosemary Butcher and Jonathan Burrows), who works from an experiential background in Alexander Technique, says: 'I wanted to come back to the essence of just the simplicity of movement, of doing very little, to later extend it into bigger phrases.'[161]

CREATIVITY AND HABITS

Movement structures in classes can be initiated by the dancer or through the agency of someone else through touch. Hands-on work, when someone is moved by another person, can create movement experiences that challenge and expose a person's movement habits. When individuals allow themselves to be moved in ways that they have not experienced before, or without their own control, it can help to break down habits and make people conscious of a greater range of possibilities for their movement.

Somatic practitioners Joan Skinner, Bonnie Bainbridge Cohen, Thomas Hanna and others all practised an approach of hands-on work to create movement in places where movement was blocked, to open up new perceptual experiences and re-integrate aspects of a person's embodiment into their consciousness again. Hanna called the act of blocking an avenue of perceptual awareness of an aspect of the body – perceptual amnesia.[162] The result of exposing limitations in our perceptual experience of ourselves opens up the possibility of increasing self-awareness, and thus the experience of perceptual processes, enabling a fuller, deeper and bigger, more conscious sense of self. Release-based teacher Alice Sara talks about her use of

SYLVIE FORTIN TALKS ABOUT ATTENTION AND HABIT

Moving our attention first requires us to notice habitual patterns that we are not aware of. Habit, some would argue, is a mechanism of efficiency. Unfortunately there is often no room for creativity in effi-ciency. Habit allows us to do something and not have to think about it, or devote much attention to it. Freeing habitual holding patterns allows us to access and express our creativity more fully. When we gain some mastery in the movement of our attention, we are learning how to experience life differently.[164]

'taking each other's weight, directing each other with that'; she continues:

We did as an introduction the sense of taking the weight of the head into each other's hands and just taking that to walk forwards into the hands. A really simple sequence of actions that we did together just to start to notice our weight and each other's weight.[163]

This form of activity can then make the dancers more aware of their head moving through space, and how they support the head as an extension of the spine. Dancers can then carry that self-aware-ness into other movement sequences without a partner's touch, sequences that have been created to explore the same attentional focus.

Fig. 95: Feeling the weight of the head. Release class taught by Melanie Clarke, featuring dancers Holly Smith and Rebecca Hunt; Trinity Laban Conservatoire of Music and Dance, London. JAMES KEATES

SALVITTI TALKS ABOUT INTEGRATION AND HABIT

Releasing often habitually held super-ficial muscles in a quiet, slow-paced class environment also gives students the opportunity to re-pattern and let go of movement habits that are no longer serving them. Dancers learn that it is not individual muscle strength that makes one strong, but putting the body into a connected relationship as a whole and with space and the ground.[165]

The focus of attention is applied to a wide-ranging exploration that provides experience and aware-ness of many possibilities. This is distinct from other technique practices that also obviously use the possibility for the body to learn patterns to instill skills, but these skills are defined within a set of parameters. In Release-based Technique the skills are not narrowed to their application to a specified selection of movement components, but specifi-cally opened up so theoretically any movement is possible. This means that all movement is equally valued, and thus there is no right or wrong way to move, there is only the choice to move this way, in this moment. Within classes there will be open exploration of motion as well as very specific move-ments to apply understanding.

The attention to awareness is used to direct the initiation of movement in specific ways through set

Fig. 96: Sensing the shoulder blades. Release class taught by Melanie Clarke, featuring dancers Luca Braccia and Alessandra Ruggeri; Trinity Laban Conservatoire of Music and Dance, London. JAMES KEATES

or improvised material. But the focus of attention can change, and a different specific application of attention will be used to initiate another specificity in moving. Gill Clarke, the highly influential Release-based Technique teacher and dancer/collaborator in the Siobhan Davies Company for many years, is quoted as saying that the on-going practice can be '…to refine the quality of attention'.[166] Sylvie Fortin claims that 'creativity is linked to our capacity to simply shift our attention to notice new options. Shifting attention is a key concept of somatic practices. We can construct a radically different world via the direction of our attention.'[167]

So there is a combination of free motion and highly specific motion in different ways. To do this, teachers are creative in their exploration of movement to generate a variety in usage of whatever theme or process is being attended to. Teachers can create phrases of movement that utilize a function of the body in as many ways as possible. For example, a teacher could employ the following measures:

- Create a class that uses focus of attention on the sensation of free rounded motion of the ball and socket joint of the hip
- Hands-on work may be used to develop awareness, as well as thoroughly warm up the joints
- There may be improvisation or set material to explore that motion in different ways, such as initiating from the hip socket, the leg moving from the hip, the pelvis moving over the hips, how the hip joints relate to the feet and the spine
- This will all be explored with a variety of approaches such as moving on the floor, moving into and out of the floor, standing, travelling, jumping, falling

Self-awareness brings with it the possibility of making choices in how we move because of an embodied understanding of the possibilities and how to enable them. In this way the practice of technique can be similar to current practices in choreography, in that there are no rules but you have to make choices in order to make anything. Creative learning is about exploring the possibilities so you can then make decisions about what you are choos-

MARINA COLLARD

Release-based teacher and choreographer Marina Collard explains the type of experiences she would generate in a class to attend to the embodied experience of the feet:

We just work with actually really feeling the relationship with the ground. That is…constant work for me for every class. We had a hook of the heel reaching back, sense of the foot spreading, how the bones of the arch might feel like, they are suspending and floating… so already we have a bouncing relationship with the ground, then we maybe go for a walk and then do the touch thing again, 'these are this and this bones, how does it feel now?', go for another walk. Just ordinariness. Then we will do it with a foot on the wall and then a foot on a partner, feeling different possible grounds so it is not just on the floor. And then we will do a little sequence when they shift the weight from one foot to another, we pad about on the feet, we try and stand on one leg, the other leg.

Of course the rest of the body is totally affected by that, as we are working with everything. What I will also do at some point is come back to that foot focus, so every day we will explore the foot in different ways. How that affects the hip, and then also at some point I would be asking them to work through that activity in improvisation as well. And that is generally with a partner supporting, so there is generally a moving with and a following and a witnessing, occasional hands on, so there is a constant dialogue between students about what they think they have understood.[168]

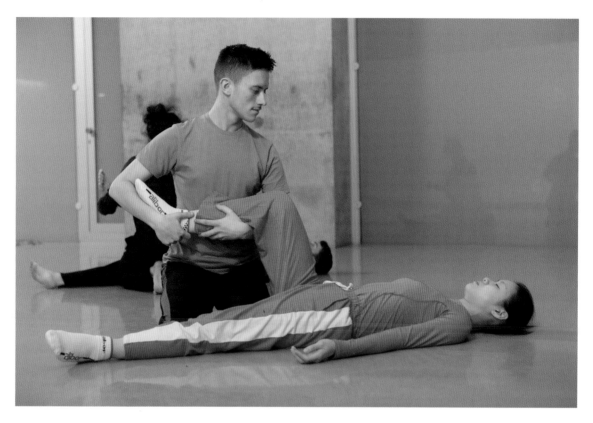

Fig. 97: Somatic hands-on practice, hip releasing. Release class taught by Melanie Clarke, featuring dancers Yu-Tzu Lin and Lewis Sharp; Trinity Laban Conservatoire of Music and Dance, London. JAMES KEATES

ing to do. This aspect of awareness of choice means that the student has to have agency to explore decision making.

This is often activated in technique classes through the use of improvisation, or through certain freedoms built into taught material, such as free timing, options for height/length/reach of the result of a movement, and individual expression. Any taught sequences of motion are created by the teacher for the purpose of using specific attentional choices. These sequences are, therefore, influenced by the individual teacher and their accumulated experiential knowledge and creativity. However, teachers have certain strategies to maintain the emphasis on individual embodiment by the students, so they are not copying the teacher and trying to be like them.

To avoid precise copying, and to encourage students to discover their embodiment of material, students are encouraged to start dancing even if they are unsure of the material, and even if they go wrong in the material to allow the exploration to continue in the moment of doing. Often there is very little 'marking' (practising for correctness by doing the movement in a small way), and doing the sequence full out with fully integrated and embodied commitment is encouraged, even if the students are not sure that they know the sequence. This method can allow the bodily process to develop an accuracy, as the clarity comes from the felt process.

The use of hands-on practice with a partner can also be used to facilitate experiencing how initiation can lead to particular sequencing, as one can direct the other from the initiating point. Methods like these support staying with the experiential process, even in learning phrases of movement material. David Waring, artistic director of Transitions Dance Company and co-programme leader of the MA Dance Performance at Trinity Laban, describes this:

Fig. 98: Individual process in class. Release class taught by Zoi Dimitriou, featuring dancers Lea Pointelin, Phoebe Hart and Simone Sistarelli; Trinity Laban Conservatoire of Music and Dance, London. JAMES KEATES

I am also letting and wanting my students to run with what I am doing. Potentially without thinking that there are really any answers, or letting that information settle with them, through them and in them to see how they connect the ideas to the next concept that we might be working with, or find other discussion points around it.[169]

A somatic approach to dance is therefore the creation of movement processes that can create attention to the perception of the body in motion to create greater awareness of, and experience of, movement possibilities. Within this approach there is an acknowledgement of each person's individuality, creative exploration and subjective assimilation of experiences. As such, classes can be seen as research into moving, where the teacher is a guide and where the student can question, decipher, explore and experiment.

BODY

In Release-based Technique the body is explored in a multi-dimensional, open way. Discovery of an individual's potential possibilities for motion, rather than particular movements, is the central aim. There is no separation between the movement, the functioning of the body in doing the movement, and the sensate, relational experience of the doer. Each student is understood to come to the learning situation with their own subjective knowledge base and personalized ways of understanding and making meaning from learning, and thus there is no assumption of any one way to do something.

Because of this there is no ideal form, process or image to pursue. Classes explore many ways into understanding and gaining knowledge about the body moving, rather than selecting one way. The

Fig. 99: Open extension and whole-body integration. Release class featuring dancer Louis Barreau; Trinity Laban Conservatoire of Music and Dance, London.

JAMES KEATES

body is explored as a functional entity, with built-in design that supports ease of motion – but that functionality always has to be the functionality of the individual rather than of an ideal, and knowledge has to be subjective, accumulated and made sense of, by the individual. Release-based Technique teacher at Trinity Laban Conservatoire of Music and Dance, and pedagogy researcher Jamieson Dryburgh, puts this as follows: 'Who one is, and what one is doing, need to be brought together.'[170]

The functionality of the body is explored through a basis in experiential anatomy, as anatomical imagery is used to relate to real aspects of the body. Attention is given to the perception of anatomical structures such as the skeleton, the fascial web, the organs, which are explored as aspects of the self in motion. Anatomical information is used as a source of individual exploration, and self-perception is used as the medium of learning. Attention is directed towards an aspect of the moving body, whether that is an area of the body, or a relationship between body areas, or the relationship of the body to the environment. For example, focus in the body can be directed to a specific body structure so that the dancer can focus on the sensate experience of that area, and use it as an initiating factor for motion, as in the example given earlier of the skull moving.

This leads to an exploration of how a movement is achieved. It is not judged on the form created, but rather, on how the intention to move is embodied and results in the movement. Conscious perception is focused to build self-awareness, but that focus does not lead to isolation. This is because the body is used as an integrated system, and every initiation is followed by a sequence of reaction through the functional tensegrity of the anatomical structures (as outlined in Chapter 2). As Marina Collard, Release-based teacher, choreographer and craniosacral therapist, says: 'The most fundamental thing is the absolute resistance to fragmentation....it is always in relationship' to the whole moving structure of the entire body.[171]

The body is explored as a tensegrity structure, which means that no one part moves without a sense of interconnection with the rest of the body,

Fig. 100: Feeling the
weight of the head.
Release class taught
by Melanie Clarke,
featuring dancer
Lewis Sharp; Trinity
Laban Conservatoire
of Music and Dance,
London. JAMES KEATES

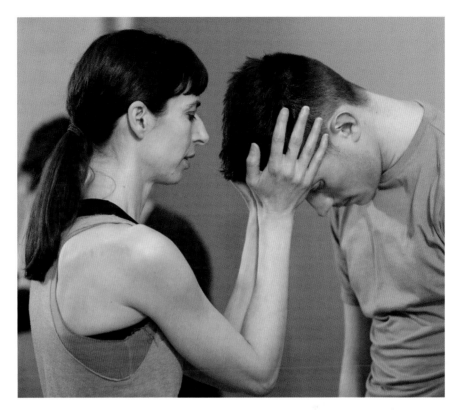

and is explored in relationship to gravity and the floor. There can be clear articulation in the joints, but with an acknowledgment of relationship across joints and through the connected structures within the body. The fascial anatomy is often a point of reference for guidance of movement initiation, which provides a basis for a purposeful and clear directing of the movement that follows. Simple movements are often a starting point for this exploration of the functionality of the body.

These simple patterns allow for clarity of attending and experiencing to support self-awareness. Henry Montes says: 'If we worked on the simplicity, on the technique of things...everything should be ready to move and you should be able to integrate more quickly.'[172] Jamieson Dryburgh says that 'having a particular focus allows us to explore through the movement what is possible, and how we might expand our awareness of, and attentiveness towards, what is possible.'[173]

Bone structure and fascial connectivity are often explored as ways to understanding the body and body relationships. The knowledge gained is experiential, but supported by theoretical underpinnings. Teachers can use model skeletons, pictures of bones and fascial connections to support understanding through visual means, but relate that to felt experience of your own body. The felt experience of movement in the joints, the relationships of bones to each other, the acknowledgement of the organs as part of movement, and the use of the fascial connections, are fundamental to the way movement is taught and should be executed. Working from the fascia enables an openness and lengthening of the joints to create freedom of motion, as well as supporting the internal perception of the body, as the fascia contains sensory nerve endings that enable proprioception and interoception.

Emphasis in Release Technique is on the experience of opening the body, and you may find that lengthening of the fascia is emphasized far more than contracting muscles. Release Technique is often practised in looser clothing than other tech-

Fig. 101: One body part leads and everything will follow. Release class taught by Melanie Clarke, featuring Melanie Clarke, Luca Braccia and Rebecca Hunt; Trinity Laban Conservatoire of Music and Dance, London. JAMES KEATES

Fig. 102: Partnering in motion. Release class taught by Melanie Clarke, featuring dancers Lewis Sharp, Alessandra Ruggeri and Luca Braccia; Trinity Laban Conservatoire of Music and Dance, London. JAMES KEATES

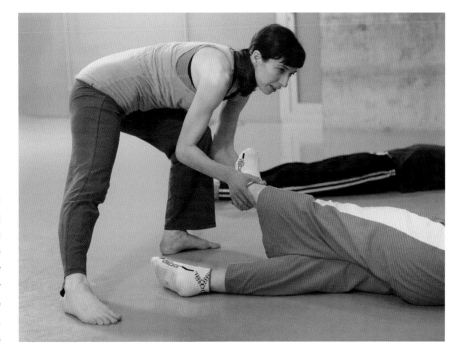

Fig. 103: Understanding sequencing through connectivity. Release class taught by Melanie Clarke; Trinity Laban Conservatoire of Music and Dance, London. JAMES KEATES

TRY THIS

Start sitting with your torso long and vertical, and your legs lengthened straight forwards in parallel, but relaxed in the muscles and feet. Then follow the sequence below:

• Tip the skull to the right until the head leads the spine into lateral (sideways) flexion
• This will open and spread the left lateral connectivity between the left ear and the left greater trochanter at the side of the top of the thigh bone (femur)
• Keep tipping the head until the spine and left lateral connectivity start to lift the left side of the pelvis
• There will be a moment of falling...
• ...then the hands catch the weight as you breathe out. The head reaches out into space, and you sequentially roll on to the belly, making a half turn so you now face the back of the space
• As you breathe in, the spine lengthens, the lungs inflate and the skull finishes slightly raised off the floor with the neck long, creating a slight hyperextension of the spine and lengthening the front surface connectivity: this is the Superficial Front Line (Myers 2014), from the top of the feet, up the front of the legs to the top front ridge of the pelvis, and from the pubic synthesis, the front of

the belly (rectus abdominis) and breast bone (sturnum), to the back of the skull (mastoid process) via the sternocleidomastoid muscles
• Then lengthen along the right leg so that the right foot crosses over the left ankle as you breathe out and release the lungs
• Keep lengthening out through the right leg and feel how that starts to turn the pelvis, which draws through the right lateral connectivity, allowing the torso to sequentially return to vertical as the sitting bones find the floor, letting the head come up last and you find yourself back in the starting position

You can try this sequencing with a partner guiding your head on the 'S'-shaped three-dimensional curve in space through the spinal flexion and extension that creates the roll to the belly. Then your partner can hold your right ankle and guide your foot across your left leg and out into space, which should draw your torso sequentially away from the floor and turn you, without you having to lift or push. Working with a partner like this can really help you feel the power of the initiation point and the sequencing through the connected body, and how easy and fluid the movement through the body can be.

niques, as tight clothing can make you more aware of the action of muscles, whereas looser clothing can make you more aware of ease of motion.

Focus on the fascial connections also supports sequencing patterns in movement where there is an initiation followed by successional motion that flows along a line of fascia. Center in Release prac-

tice is a fascial one: the relationship between the feet and skull through the deepest layers of connective tissue, musculature and organs in the body (the 'apple core' from Chapter 2, called the 'Deep Front Line' by Myers 2014). The integration of the core to all movement is considered fundamental to integrated movement.

SPACE

GENERAL SPACE/SHARED SPACE

The use of the studio space for Released-based Technique is quite specific. There is a conscious reduction in the hierarchy of the learning space so that everyone's experience is equally valued, and the teacher is seen as a guide to the dancer's exploration, rather than as the model of authority and correctness. This is at times visible in the use of space, in that the teacher may be amongst the students, or the orientation in the studio space might change so there is no set front (often facilitated by using studios without mirrors), or all may face in towards the centre of the room.

Also, the teacher often moves with the students, equally as involved in the experiencing process, verbalizing the attentional focus as they go to guide the exploration. As technique teacher and dance scientist Tina Krasevec says: 'In order to get them in the right zone I feel I have to do it with them....so that I am experiencing things with my own body to see how things change.'[174]

This process can remove the fear of going wrong, as no one is correcting or pointing out inaccuracies in individuals' processes. Because the teacher is active they often use the term 'we' when verbalizing the process engaged with (as is visible in the quotations from teachers included in this chapter). Jamieson Dryburgh says that he likes 'encouraging risk by recognizing that I need to develop, or we need to develop together, a safe space where risk and exploration is possible.'[175] However, this approach relies on the student dancers being engaged in the practice and in the felt sensation of their own experience.

Fig. 104: Working in circles with no set front. Release class taught by Melanie Clarke, featuring Melanie Clarke, Luca Braccia and Rebecca Hunt; Trinity Laban Conservatoire of Music and Dance, London. JAMES KEATES

Fig. 105: Teacher as participator in the practice. Release class taught by Melanie Clarke, featuring Melanie Clarke and Luca Braccia; Trinity Laban Conservatoire of Music and Dance, London. JAMES KEATES

Fig. 106: Using the floor. Release class taught by Melanie Clarke, featuring Melanie Clarke, Luca Braccia and Rebecca Hunt; Trinity Laban Conservatoire of Music and Dance, London. JAMES KEATES

It also requires a mental stamina, as the student has to focus their attention for themselves, and not for the approval of the teacher, and so must find an *intrinsic* (self-determined, volitional) motivation. This method of teaching permits going wrong or making mistakes in the process of discovery. The permission to not be perfect can be very freeing, as the idea of judging what you are doing is removed or at least lessened in attention. As Release-based teacher, dancer for Rosemary Butcher and choreographer, Rahel Vonmoos says: 'I try to undo hierarchy, in a way, within the moving and within the exercises or phrases or jumps or whatever, but also within that teacher/student role.'[176] As Batson states of somatic practices: 'The general aim is to induce a more relaxed state of mind in order to attend without excess anxiety and distraction.'[177]

It is a case of experiencing the movement with this specific attention, and exploring how that is enabling you to move like this, that leads to accuracy and clarity in the movement. What can be judged in this practice is the students' ability to find the intrinsic motivation, the attention and stamina of attention, and the ability to work with perception to facilitate a deep experiential process. Teachers state that the depth of process gives the work its meaning, and this can readily be seen when people move. The clarity of attention to the 'how' of the movement, the focus on perception of sensation, the initiation and subsequent sequencing, and how that leads to fluency, integrated embodiment and presence, then becomes the performance of the movement. David Waring says that the technique presents:

> ...*ideas which demand that you are present in and with what you are doing, then it is very hard not to be aware, because I think these principles necessitate a process and an engagement with a process of moving as you are moving. So you could jump ahead, you could assume that something is this or that in any given moment, but actually if you are not fulfilling the thinking of that as you do it, then somehow it will appear more superficial.*[178]

USE OF THE FLOOR

Much use is made of the support of the floor in this technique. Lying on the floor is a frequent occurrence in this practice. Lying down allows for a releasing of tension and holding as the floor provides a total support for the body. There is a lying posture that comes from Alexander Technique called recuperative rest, where you lie supine (on your back) with your knees bent and your feet on the floor; this

Fig. 107: Starting from the recuperative rest position. Release class taught by Zoi Dimitriou, featuring dancer Zoi Dimitriou (standing); Trinity Laban Conservatoire of Music and Dance, London. JAMES KEATES

Fig. 108: Using the floor for support. Release class taught by Zoi Dimitriou, featuring dancers Samantha Furnival, Phoebe Hart and Danielle Evans; Trinity Laban Conservatoire of Music and Dance, London. JAMES KEATES

posture helps the spine lengthen, the weight of the pelvis release into the floor, the chest soften and open, the neck release as the weight of the head is supported, and the shoulder blades release.

There is focused attention on releasing and letting go into the floor, a yielding of bodyweight. The release of the body into the total support of the ground creates a distribution of weight through all the body surfaces touching the floor, and supports integrated energy through the body. Support from the floor without gripping or holding then allows for any lifting or reaching out with parts of the body to be supported through a distribution of weight through the whole integrated structure.

A body part initiating by reaching out then leads to a sequencing motion in the body, transference of weight into new surfaces, and motion in space (as in the example above). Relationships through the body found on the floor can then be re-found in standing work – even though the relationship to gravity may shift by ninety degrees, the integration of the body, the distribution of effort and the sequencing from a point of initiation through the connected integration, is the same.

USE OF THE KINESPHERE

The emphasis on how a movement becomes manifested by the body leads to an emphasis on pathway, and thus what is termed in choreological practice 'spatial progression'. The sequencing and fluency in Release-based work can create a sequence of motion that emphasizes the flow, rather than the destinational result of movement. It does not mean that there is no destination – movement can still have clear spatial definition – but the destination is not a fixed point and is not emphasized. Movement then continues fluently into the next initiation and sequencing that can stem from the initial pathway.

This is distinct from Cunningham and Graham, where, even though the movement is in the motion, the destinational form and shape is made visible in the performance. In release, the beginning of a motion, the initiation, can have more focus than the destination, as the precision of initiation then

Fig. 109: Lability. Release class taught by Zoi Dimitriou, featuring dancer Silvio Sighinolfi; Trinity Laban Conservatoire of Music and Dance, London.
JAMES KEATES

allows for the sequencing that creates the pathway. Pathways in Release-based Technique can often be circular or curved. This emphasizes how the body works: the body has many centres, and when we move with a relationship between centre and periphery, then we move on curved paths. Also, the curve of pathways allows for and supports the fluency of motion, as circles have no end.

The use of curves and circles can also allow for build-up of momentum, in that releasing weight into a curved pathway can increase speed and create swing. Just like the letting go of the body completely leads to a rapid falling to the earth in gravity, the swing of weight on a curve uses mass in gravity to create momentum in a pattern of increasing and then decreasing speed. Circular pathways, particularly peripheral ones, can create a felt experience of the relationship between the body centre and the body periphery, which supports bodily integration. Integration, swing and momentum are vital for fluency and speed in floor work, for example, which can be a feature of some release classes or classes that have evolved from this approach.

This swing of weight is known as *fall and recovery* in the technique and practice of early modern dance pioneer Doris Humphrey, which was taken up by her student Jose Limon and became known as 'Humphrey Limon Technique'. Thus, use of swing means that there can be some similarities between Humphrey-Limon and some movements within Release-based Techniques. However, curved pathways in Release can be used with a full range of rhythmic and dynamic possibilities, as exploring wide possibilities is a key feature of the approach, and the use of swing can be a choice rather than a feature of the practice.

THE SPACE IN THE BODY

Space is also considered as an elastic property of the body. David Waring says: 'Somehow it has got to be about the realization of the space in the body and the body in space.'[179] The body is viewed as an elastic structure that can change in size and shape based on the flux that comes from breath-

Fig. 110: Feeling the breath in the body. Release class taught by Melanie Clarke, featuring dancer Luca Braccia; Trinity Laban Conservatoire of Music and Dance, London. JAMES KEATES

ing. The expanding and then shrinking of the volume of the lungs in breathing, and how the motion of that creates fluctuations through the body, can be viewed as a property of space. Our torso literally changes shape as we breathe. Allowing breath to be full and deep then starts to open up our awareness of the range of movement possibilities in three-dimensional space.

Fig. 111: Elevation. Release class taught by Melanie Clarke, featuring dancer Luca Braccia; Trinity Laban Conservatoire of Music and Dance, London. JAMES KEATES

The use of breath then becomes an important and integrated part of the practice. Breath can be the initiator of movement, the inhale creating volumous support for any lifting and opening energy in the upper body, involving the lungs, ribs and spine into arm movements as one integrated expression. The exhale can support flexion of the spine, movement inwards and movement with releasing into gravity. Integrating breathing and moving integrates the layers of the body into one expressive action.

Henry Montes claims that if students 'really utilize the breath, it really is transformative.'[180] The work of the Laban/Bartenieff Institute of Movement highlights the awareness of the breath in terms of growing and shrinking in the body, which is known as 'shape flow'. The integrated use of the breath to support physical action in space is known as 'shape change'. Peggy Hackney describes breath as a 'key to fluidity of movement, internal shaping, the experience of inner space as three-dimensional.'[181] As Marina Collard says:

If you make space in the body and people start breathing they feel a lot better...but what it does is it brings them into their body and

Fig. 112: Three-dimensional use of space. Release class taught by Melanie Clarke, featuring dancer Yu-Tzu Lin; Trinity Laban Conservatoire of Music and Dance, London. JAMES KEATES

into relationship with what it is they are doing and what they are working with, which is themselves.[182]

The focus on experiencing your anatomy also brings awareness to the volume of the body in space, and the curves and rounded forms of the body. The body is not conceived of as lines, superimposing images of straightness. The bones, and the fascial connectivity that gives the body shape around the bones, undulate and curve. The felt experience of the shape of the body, and the body's relationship to space, is a sensorial understanding. The sense of spatial progression within the technique can also be within the space of the body, and not just in the space around the body.

Movement can progress from initiation through a sequence that is given form through internal bodily structures the result of which is expressed outwardly. Henry Montes says: 'It is spatial, but it is the spherically of the body',[183] meaning that movement is conceived of as rounded and three dimensional. The point of attentional focus can roam along bodily structures and find three-dimensional form. It is again about potentiality and the need for the experience of moving, rather than an ease of quantifying movement to be the focus, and thus can be an unfragmented use of space.

Choice in the use of spatial form, such as extension into dimensions (the *vertical dimension*, which is the vertical line up to down, the *lateral dimension*, which is right to left, and the *sagittal dimension*, which is forwards to backwards) and focus on planes of motion (the horizontal or *table plane* that interconnects, the sagittal dimension with the lateral, the vertical or *door plane* that interconnects the vertical and lateral dimensions, and the sagittal or *wheel plane* that interconnects the vertical and sagitta dimensions) is utilized.

However, movement can spiral, turn and change orientation during an on-going progression, creating three-dimensional skew curves and complex forms that are difficult to describe spatially in simple terms, but possible to feel as pathways through the body. As Henry Montes again describes: 'I can

MOVEMENT IN ANY POSSIBLE DIRECTION

David Waring says: Because the body has the potential for balance and ease of balance if it is unrestricted, then that to me is what gives it the potential to go in any direction we want to or where we send it; how, of course, we find the different supports, anchors to make that happen or not, to just allow the body to go towards the fall, is what is extremely interesting to me.[185]

sense the spiralling down, and I can sense from the ground the spiralling up.'[184]

ACTION

The actions of the body in this technique can be wide and various and changing. Range of motion in the body is purposefully explored without any hierarchy of what aspects of range could be more desired or more important – thus all possibilities are considered and valued equally. Often classes can focus attention on an aspect of the body in order to be able to explore many and various possibilities for that aspect, but when the focus changes, the class structure and movement used changes. As stated previously, it is the approach to learning that qualifies the umbrella title of this technique, rather than the movement vocabulary. This is distinct from the techniques already discussed, which maintain a selected set of principles and a certain adherence to structure and vocabulary over time, even though the specific construction and selection of exercises and sequences may vary from class to class. The parameters for attention with Release-based Technique practices offer width and depth of exploration by creating limitation of focus.

Fig. 113: Leading from the skull. Release class taught by Melanie Clarke, featuring dancers Yu-Tzu Lin and Lewis Sharp; Trinity Laban Conservatoire of Music and Dance, London. JAMES KEATES

The simple patterns of movement used to promote self-awareness and the practice of functional patterning can include developmental patterns following the work of Bonnie Bainbridge Cohen in Body-Mind Centering (Irmgard Bartenieff and Peggy Hackney in Bartenieff Fundamentals utilize similar patterns called 'fundamental patterns of total body connectivity'). Developmental patterns are the movements that babies explore unconsciously as they learn to sense and move their bodies. Developmental patterns can also be related to animal movement patterns following an evolutionary journey from single-celled organism, to vertebrates, to amphibian locomotion, to quadrupedal locomotion. Bonnie Bainbridge Cohen articulates the developmental patterns as:

The first of the four prevertebrate patterns is cellular breathing *(the expanding/contracting process in breathing and movement in each and every cell of the body), which correlates to the movement of the one-celled animals....*

Navel radiation *(the relating and movement of all parts of the body via the navel),* mouthing *(movement of the body initiated by the mouth), and* prespinal movement *(soft sequential movements of the spine initiated via the interface between spinal cord and the digestive tract) are the other three prevertebrate patterns.*

The twelve vertebrate patterns are based upon spinal movement *(head-to-tail movement), which correlates to the movement of fish;* homologous movement *(symmetrical movement of two upper and/or two lower limbs simultaneously), which correlates to the movement of amphibians;* homolateral movement *(asymmetrical movement of one upper limb and the lower limb on the same side), which correlates to the movement of reptiles; and* contralateral movement *(diagonal movement of one upper limb with the opposite lower limb), which correlates to the movement of mammals.'*[186]

Fig. 114: Spinal movement. Release class taught by Melanie Clarke, featuring Melanie Clarke, Luca Braccia and Rebecca Hunt; Trinity Laban Conservatoire of Music and Dance, London. JAMES KEATES

RELEASE-BASED TECHNIQUE TERMINOLOGY

Connectivity Pattern

Myers	Deep front line, superficial front line, superficial back line	Lateral lines	Functional lines	All the lines
Hackney	Upper/lower connectivity	Homolateral/ body halves	Cross-lateral	Core-distal connectivity
Bainbridge Cohen	Spinal movement/ head to tail	Homolateral movement	Contralateral movement	Navel radiation

Classes can explore these patterns, usually initially on the floor, and then use them in sequences of motion. These sequences of motion follow certain pathways due to the structural interconnectivity of the body. Release-based classes use these patterns and pathways to enable a more conscious recognition of the experience of these sequences. In this way you can become more physically aware of these functional processes that enable movement and support ease of motion. Experiential knowing of these movement particulars is applied to or embedded into dance phrases, enabling the person to experience the relevance of these patterns for ease and clarity of motion in dance. Hackney says that 'Each fundamental pattern of total body connectivity represents a primary level of development and experience and each is rela-tional. Each organizes a way of relating to self and to the world.'[187]

Table 1 relates three sets of terminology for these patterns that can be applied in Release-based Technique classes: these come from the work of Thomas Myers,[188] Peggy Hackney[189] and Bonnie Bainbridge Cohen.[190]

Within the explorations of integrated movement there is no holding of shape around the action; for example, a shaping in the arms is not held whilst other movements are done, which can be common in ballet and in Cunningham and Graham Techniques. Thus the aim of the motion is all the movement that is done; energy is not given to anything outside, or in addition to, the movement being performed. As can be seen in Figure 115, one arm is allowed to hang passively whilst energy is committed to the expressive fulfilment of a lengthening initiated by the other arm, and integrated through the cross-lateral connectivity.

These actions, therefore, are not framed by another part of the body. This means that the body is doing

Fig. 115: Reach and extending into space. Release class taught by Melanie Clarke, featuring Melanie Clarke, Holly Smith; Trinity Laban Conservatoire of Music and Dance, London. JAMES KEATES

one thing, which may be fully integrated through the entire body or following a particular trajectory, whilst other aspects of the body are passive. There is a voluntary reduction of effort in the body through the releasing of tension and commitment outside the purpose of the action. The conscious reduction is a controlled function, but creates an efficiency of energetic usage in the musculature. This is practised in simple actions and through the use of the floor as a support for the whole body.

Efficiency in the use of energy is also gained from the utilization of sequencing; the initiation of movement is energy full, but there is no need to lift or hold against gravity in the movement that follows. Through an organic balancing of energies, such as reaching out and the balancing of that through drawing in, opening and closing, expanding and reducing, a physical elastic flux, connected to breathing, is generated, which creates balance of usage throughout the body and a distribution of effort.

Movement patterns used to support awareness of body integration and connection are more uniformly shared across teachers' practices, but how these are used in sequences of motion in classes is often complex and individualized. The idea is that once the experiential understanding of a pattern, function and inter-relationship is generated it can be accessed in complex motion, shifting the approach. At first clarity of attention supported by somatic focus can lead to body action, but then the motion is allowed to lead, and the mind follows the flow of the movement through an experiential reflection. As Release-based teacher, Alice Sara says: 'Whenever there is more mindful slower, attentive somatic work, I want that to open up possibilities to then trust in the going, doing and the playing'.[191] Marina Collard explains:

Fig. 116: Flow of motion. Release class taught by Zoi Dimitriou, featuring dancers Phoebe Hart, Louis Barreau, Mathilde Lepage-Bagatta and Simone Sistarelli; Trinity Laban Conservatoire of Music and Dance, London. JAMES KEATES

I want them to learn to move and to be able to move with absolute precision and absolute freedom. The only way that can happen, I think, is that they are embodied in that moment of doing so they are just following. So the brain is almost that hair of a tiny fraction behind and listening and following.[192]

This process of allowing the body to lead can be done through improvisation or set movement sequences, where the focus remains on the sensation of the movement happening. As Sara Reed claims:

This method of learning is not about the correct execution of form....learning in and through somatic practices relates to the qualities of these sensations experienced, which dancers may then go on to develop and use.[193]

The emphasis is not on correctness of the form, but how it is approached: discovery and exploration is the aim, rather than accuracy. This supports the opportunity for complexity in bodily and spatial form, as the movement does not need to be divisible, quantified and named. That does not mean, however, that accuracy is not achieved: accuracy is a result of clarity in the process of initiation and sequencing through the body, but that accuracy does not necessarily have a spatial stopping point or defined shape. Initiated movement can continue until something else is initiated from it. For example, reaching out can continue until it pulls the body off balance, leading to a fall, which leads to flow of weight and rebalancing in some way that initiates something else. As Marina Collard describes:

There is always decision making because you know where you are, it is always responsive and aware. But you are not contriving, it is not a pre-planned thing, it goes too fast for that to happen. The body, trusting the embodied presence, is a particular kind of thinking as moving, which works much faster than the brain, and that is kind of what I want them

to realize. Their own innate intelligence, the astute listening, once the body is well organized, is much faster, it resolves stuff much more quickly than the brain, even in picking up material.[194]

So there is a reliance on the perceptual information that flows to the brain to create a reaction, and an embodied understanding of the flow of motion through the body, and how that creates a sequence of events. This means that the motion does not have to be mentally divided into that many separate parts, and the flow creates a bodily logic for why one initiation leads to the next one. Movement then does not have to be in discrete units, and becomes more fluid and flowing phrases of action and reaction. For example: a turning of the heel on the floor can lead to a sequence of energy travelling up through the leg into and onwards up through the spine, lengthening up into the head, until it makes the head tip sideward, which causes the weight to fall into one body half with a lowering of weight which drops the weight of the head and changes the spine which changes the orientation; this brings the other body half after it, which creates a transference of weight, shifting weight to the other body half; this brings the hand to the floor, which supports a further lowering of the centre of gravity with a sagittal shift in space as the support of the feet transfers to the pelvis.

As can be seen in the above example, the clarity of the first initiation and how that creates a sequencing then becomes paramount in facilitation of the entire

MOVEMENT COMPLEXITY

Nelson says: 'I can perceive the experience of my body's movement, but cannot fully understand its infinite possibility.'[195]

Fig. 117: Moving on the floor. Release class taught by Melanie Clarke, featuring dancer Luca Braccia; Trinity Laban Conservatoire of Music and Dance, London. JAMES KEATES

JAMIESON DRYBURGH'S APPROACH

The movement material is just the vehicle through which we are exploring. So the movement material is *almost* irrelevant. And although it tends to be the thing that a lot of people fixate on, for me it's just stuff through which we draw our attention to particular functions of the body or particular articulations of the body. And so the way I plan a session is that there is a central idea or theme which I think will be useful for us to explore, and which is usually very bodily focused. For example, it might be the way in which the shoulder blades slide on the ribcage, which allows the arm to extend, and through extending the arm from the shoulder blade how movement might follow. So, that very simple idea might be explored in lots of different ways:

- in a very simplistic improvisation: let's slide the shoulder blade on the ribcage

- it might be through partner work or hands-on, feeling how it is working on other people's bodies, and using the touch to be able to facilitate a greater awareness of where the shoulder blades are placed on the body
- it comes through talk and discussion about all those things we are experiencing, and trying to capture something about embodied knowing through language
- and then it comes through having more complex sequences of movement that might be very pleasurable to dance or very expansive in the space, but which draw our attention to the work of the shoulder blade on the ribcage

So, having a particular focus allows us to explore through the movement what is possible, and how we might expand our awareness and attentiveness towards what is possible.[196]

Fig. 118: Using touch to guide attention. Release class taught by Melanie Clarke, featuring dancers Luca Braccia, Holly Smith, Lewis Sharp and Rebecca Hunt; Trinity Laban Conservatoire of Music and Dance, London. JAMES KEATES

sequential flow of this one phrase of movement. The example also reveals the complexity of spatial path, and how at first the pathway is in the body with an upwards and then lateral flow, but eventually comes out into forward motion in the space, even though that forward has changed from the starting orientation.

DYNAMICS

The approach to learning used in Release-based classes supports a certain range of energy usage. The pared-down movement language used for its

somatic function with its unforced pace, the calm learning environment and focused attention have some dynamic particularities. A quietness is needed to be able to focus the attention, which can lead to less focus on time. The felt sensorial experience provides a sense of the bodyweight and balance of forces. A soft quality comes from the use of touch between people, and between the body and the floor through the yielding of weight and lack of superficial tension and holding patterns. The connection to breath and relationship to organs opens the potential for feeling and use of flow. The open relationship

Fig. 119: Lability. Release class taught by Melanie Clarke, featuring dancer Luca Braccia; Trinity Laban Conservatoire of Music and Dance, London.

JAMES KEATES

to space supports an outward flow of energy, which engages a free flow quality supported by the use of working with and not resisting gravity.

There is muscular work in the body, otherwise there would be no movement; however, the inter-relationship and interconnection of movement in the body means that muscular energy is spread and not held in parts, and thus is potentially less visible. Ease of mobility in the joints with the focus on path-way and curve leads to an indirect or flexible atten-tion to space. Free flow and flexible use of space creates an open fluidity in performance.

The connection of the breath to movement can bring a fulfilment of expression from the inside out, although this is not attached to any narrative or imagination structure. Finding breath support and shape flow in the plasticity of the movement of the body leads to continued changes in degrees of different dynamic energies. Degrees of free flow can change frequently, particularly in the use of the elas-tic lengthening of the fascia followed by intentional releasing, particularly when that energy comes from the changing volume in the lungs.

Working with gravity can also lead to what is termed *lability* in choreological practice. Lability is the relational interplay between falling and stabil-ity when the weight is in motion. Use of lability can be within the felt experience of the body through an internally felt weight transference or shift in weight distribution (as in the movement phrase exam-ple above). This sensation can lead to a fluency of weight through the use of falling, which can lead to a fluency in motion through space. Strength as a dynamic is not generally emphasized in movement: there can be a strong press into the floor, but this is not done with the fast bound energy in Graham Technique, and tends to be rather through the yield-ing of weight, which then transforms into a slower pushing away or a buoyancy based on the spring of connectivity rather than force, or the use of fall and lability to provide momentum. Marina Collard says:

They can listen to their body and their weight, then the dynamics will come from that. I am not imposing or putting another something on

Fig. 120: Using touch to provide information. Release class taught by Melanie Clarke, featuring Melanie Clarke; Trinity Laban Conservatoire of Music and Dance, London. JAMES KEATES

material, but demanding that they notice the dynamic, energetic necessity that emerges from the embodiment of the movement, and how they manage their weight and physicality within that. That is what I try and get. Sometimes I do things that might be rhythmic...I address weight as being something that is constantly changing and textured, and buoyant and live in its relationship. The point when you can let your weight bob about in the space the rhythm will find itself.[197]

In more complex sequences of movement, energy is committed into the focus of the movement performed, which can utilize a wide range of dynamics – but these qualities may be in constant change in the flow of the motion. Sequences need not be soft or so organically connected. Sequences can include changes of time in terms of speeding up and slowing down, as they are not tied to musical rhythm, for example, or can purposefully be broken with stillness.

Conversely, continuousness in which there is a conscious lack of rhythmic change can be practised to emphasize the fluid on-goingness and spatial progression, even if that means purposefully negating the natural rhythms that would come with the use of gravity, such as impulse/decelerating energy to go up, and impact/accelerating energy to go down. In these ways time can become a far greater presence, creating a mobility and possibility of conscious change.

Commitment of weight to general space, which can bring with it a sense of push, can be brought back into fluidity of weight in the body within one phrase of motion. Thus dynamics are not necessarily statements within a class, but become as fluid and on-going, and ever changing, as other aspects of the technique. Bonnie Bainbridge Cohen says:

Our body moves as our mind moves. The qualities of any movement are a manifestation of how mind is expressing through the body at that moment. Changes in movement qualities indicate that the mind has shifted focus in the body. Conversely, when we direct the mind or attention to different areas of the body and initiate movement from those areas, we change the quality of our movement.[198]

RELATIONSHIPS

RELATIONSHIP TO THE ENVIRONMENT

Marina Collard comments: '..[Dancing] is never on our own, basically. If you are dancing a solo you are still dancing with the floor.'[199]

Relationship is a key term in Release-based work, as the body is conceived as a whole system of interconnection. Furthermore, the relationship of perception of self to perception of environment is actively attended to. One aspect of that environment is the floor, and that relationship is explored very fully through a full range of supporting surfaces, motion on, into and out of the floor being very typical in classes, as previously described.

Another aspect of the relationship to environment is that it includes other people. Dance learning is primarily done in group learning situations, and there is an opportunity to use the presence of each other in the learning process very constructively. As Marina Collard says: 'We are not working on our own. I learn within the context of other people learning what that is for them. I see other people in the space'.[200] Alice Sara, Rahel Vonmoos, Marina Collard and Tina Krasevec (personal communications) describe students witnessing each other as an activity within the class.

The act of active watching reassigns the student as the witness or viewer creating a relationship structure related to the idea of having a reciprocal relationship to an audience. Just the fact of being watched changes the movement practice to a performance through the awareness of being seen – which means the act of awareness of self in motion is simultaneous with the awareness that what you are doing can be seen. Jamieson Dryburgh says: 'There is something important about presence and being confident enough to let people see you, and also about being connected to the environment and knowing that the environment contains an audience.'[201]

Students actively watching each other in a supportive way, and then discussing what they witness with each other, further breaks down the traditional hierarchies of dance learning that are

Fig. 121: Witnessing. Release class taught by Zoi Dimitriou, featuring dancers Alice Lebant and Valeria Famularo; Trinity Laban Conservatoire of Music and Dance, London. JAMES KEATES

established in the use of the space. The teacher is not the only person who can provide feedback, and this acknowledges the knowledge that the students themselves bring to the class, and the fact that they are active agents in their own learning – although Alice Sara says: 'It is almost less about the actual feedback and the giving of it, as it is about the watching and having someone to share with.'[202]

In this way teacher and student voices are entwined within the practice of learning, and everyone has a voice.[203] This relates to the idea of being open to sharing, which also comes into the relationship to the environment in that you let the environment in, the light comes to your eyes, the floor meets you, the space moulds you. You are open to the space rather than commanding the space. This relates to a performance mode where the audience is as equal a presence as the performer. The performer invites the audience's attention, rather than trying to grab it.

TOUCH

Contact between people is also a feature of the technique. 'Hands-on work' is a term frequently used to indicate how touch can support self-aware-ness. Contact between body and floor, body and the same body, and body and other body are all

EXPERIENCING ANATOMY THROUGH TOUCH AND SENSATION

Marina Collard says: I'll obsess with a particular detail in the body and we will approach that in all kinds of ways. Some of it might be just really touching it, touching it in partners, thinking, feel-ing, moving together, noticing, doing it again, the repetition of understanding the anatomy.[204]

utilized as ways of creating perceptual experiences. So students can be asked to touch themselves, to touch others, and to become aware of their contact with the floor.

Fig. 122: Using touch. Release class taught by Melanie Clarke, featuring dancers Luca Braccia and Alessandra Ruggeri; Trinity Laban Conservatoire of Music and Dance, London. JAMES KEATES

Touch provides a relational experience between the internal perceptual systems and the environment, whether that is a surface or another person. By stimulating the receptors in the skin, and the feedback channels through the nervous system, experiential information is obtained. Contact becomes an experience of selfhood, in that you perceive the edges of your body from the inside, and simultaneously perceive your relationship to the world outside of you in that you meet the outside through that same structure. As Bonnie Bainbridge Cohen says:

Through our skin, we touch and are touched by the outer world. The outer boundary is our first line of defence and bonding. It sets our general tone of openness and closeness to being in the world – through our skin we are both invaded and protected, and we receive and make contact with others.[205]

Touch is also a way of generating and/or sensing a moving experience for the body, where the control and the habitual patterns that lead to that

Fig. 123: Somatic hands-on practice. Release class taught by Melanie Clarke, featuring dancers Holly Smith and Rebecca Hunt; Trinity Laban Conservatoire of Music and Dance, London.
JAMES KEATES

control are taken away: one person can use touch to move someone else. In this process the person being moved has to relinquish a certain amount of physical control, dependent on what is being moved and whether they are lying down or standing. This process can be done lying down to help facilitate the non-doing, as the floor supports the weight of the body completely. When standing, the person has to maintain a sense of some balance, as they must still enable themselves to not fall over whilst being moved. Perception of the body moving then follows the motion that is happening through a letting go of a certain amount of control.

These processes can help to re-pattern movement responses through experiencing different ways of moving. For example, someone can support someone else's arm in order to mobilize their shoulder girdle, which provides the connections through the skeleton, fascia and musculature in the upper torso that allow for the range of motion possibilities for the arm beyond the actions of the shoulder joint, elbow and wrist alone. The skeletal landmarks of the shoulder girdle are the shoulder blade (scapular) that slides in the upper back, and the collar bones (clavicle) that rotate in a dynamic relationship with the breast bone (sternum) and the shoulder joint (glenohumoral joint).

The person being moved needs to let go the control of their arm through a conscious non-doing, whilst maintaining their equilibrium. Equilibrium is used here rather than stability, as there may be resultant motion of the whole body through the influence of the moving part, which means that the free motion is in relationship to the whole body, and there is no holding or fixing.

The awareness that can stem from this activity is an experiential encounter with a freedom of motion and an ease of motion that has no purposeful expression in form: that is, it is not tied to a movement result, but rather exists as an exploration of possibilities. The information received from this experience can then be used to support self-awareness and awareness of movement potential to facilitate free motion, ease and clarity, whether that is done through improvisation or movement sequences.

This hands-on activity is also relational, as it is not one-sided; the mover also has to find ways to support and manipulate someone else whilst maintaining their own equilibrium. If they are moving someone else in a three-dimensional exploration through the use of their own body, then they are also gaining an experience and exploring space, in a way that has no set form or destination. Moreover, they are feeling the motion of the other person through the medium of touch, and seeing the results of their movement on another. Thus, the person controlling the movement is also having a movement experience, which is physical exercise, exploration of the three dimensionality of the body, and an exercise in different qualities of touch.

As Bonnie Bainbridge Cohen says: 'When we touch someone, they touch us equally.'[206] The experience of your effect on the external environment and the external environment's effect on you, through touch, can provide experience of different dynamic qualities, and the idea of 'touching the space' can help the sense of qualitative motion. As Rahel Vonmoos says: 'Sometimes the touch, it is kind of like an art itself, how to touch.'[207]

Hands-on processes take time, as accessing the non-doing takes focus, which has to be found, and the process of exploration needs long enough to be full, and the process needs to be reciprocated as partners swap roles. Time in classes is used for these processes in order to develop the knowledge and experiences required. Even though this means there is less time spent in a class on taught sequences of movement, the somatic process enables a more efficient practice, as the skills to do the choreographed movement phrases when they come, are already enabled. Also, the somatic processes thoroughly warm and prepare the body for motion, so you can go directly from hand-on work to full improvisation to complex sequences without the requirement for more formal exercises to warm up and instill skills.

DIALOGUE

As stated above, these processes of relational and reciprocal activity are often followed by dialogue

ALICE SARA'S APPROACH

I have started doing more of opening up some discussions with the whole group, after they have done something a bit more explorative – maybe 'How was that?' kind of questions, or 'What did you notice?'. Sometimes we might do a kind of comparative task, maybe even with some material, for example, simply like a task with eyes closed and then a task with eyes open, and then ask: 'How did it feel different?', or 'What was different about that?'. The other day we did something with a sense of initiating from our core, or initiating from our periphery, then asked: 'What was the difference between that?', 'What did you find valuable about either one?' – and noticed that some people benefited more from one than the other.

Then at other times I might use dialogue for problem solving: maybe, later on in the class, when we are doing some more complex phrase, I ask them firstly, 'What

bits are problematic?' or 'What are we finding difficult here, how might we solve them?' Or I ask them to share what they are finding useful: 'What are people finding helpful here/ what is a hindrance here, what are we thinking about?' Sometimes they are just picking up from feedback I have given previously, at other times they are finding things that I haven't thought of, or it feels like a kind of group problem solving.

It seems to be quite good for motivation....Bringing everybody together...valuing each voice and helping them actually realize what I am teaching them: you need to use that information, so you are not just experiencing that and then dancing and hoping for the best, you can actually take hold of some of that....your own previous experience and observations that you can then, having reflected on them, apply to something.[210]

between the partners to discuss their experiences. These dialogues are also often promoted features within a release class. Jamieson Dryburgh uses dialogue very purposefully as part of the class process:

In this idea of bringing attentiveness to what we are doing I am using a whole load of strategies, and the most important for me is dialogue. It is actually trying to find a way of articulating what is going on in their body. Ultimately it is for themselves, but the way in which we discover it is through trying to say it to each other: 'This thing is going on for me right now'.[208]

David Waring reconfirms this: 'I am also asking the students to articulate their thoughts, ideas and observations in and of themselves and others in order to broaden the dialogue.'[209]

MUSIC OR SOUND

Music can also be explored in many different ways, and individual teachers may have certain preferences in the use of time as a component of movement and in relation to music. Classes may use pre-recorded music, or have a musician playing live accompaniment. Open structures can be incorporated into classes, such as free timing for movement phrases when the motion is purposefully not

Fig. 124: Improvisation in technique class. Release class taught by Melanie Clarke, featuring dancer Luca Braccia; Trinity Laban Conservatoire of Music and Dance, London. JAMES KEATES

connected to metric time structures. Perhaps a pulse is established for a sequence but counts are not given, or sound accompaniment does not have an audible beat. This can encourage individuals to find an individual feeling for the timing of the motion in their own body, rather than trying to meet an audible time structure.

Not thinking about counts can also support the clarity of attention on the bodily experience, as thinking is not divided. Some things may be done in silence, with the teacher's voice leading the group process, rather than musical phrasing. Improvisation is also often incorporated in classes so that dancers can explore movement principles within an idiosyncratic movement language (and without the need to memorize set vocabulary) and explore

their own timing and/or response to music. Marina Collard says:

> I sometimes set counts, but I am more likely to set a meter that is driving something....We get much more than just a meter from the sound, so they need to consider what they are actually listening to – the richness of layered sound coming from the musician, what choices they are making in relation to that.[211]

Some teachers set counts to explore the feeling of moving together as a group, supporting the relationship of group process. Others may focus more on allowing free, personalized timing, where individuals can be different and separate in time. Often there can be a combination of both of these approaches in one class, or it can change according to the attentional focus and the material that comes from that. When a pulse is used it can often be a three-four time signature that is selected, where each 'count' is actually the phrase of one bar of music. This is used to support and emphasize the time between beats, which corresponds to the focus on sequencing and progression of motion as well as the lack of hitting a destination.

STRUCTURES OF A RELEASE-BASED CLASS

In classes, exploration of technical principles with a focus on the embodied sensation and internal perception is combined with sequences of fluent motion. There may be fewer set exercises than in other technical forms, so less to remember, but more explorative questions and sensorial experiences. Class structures and processes may change according to the attentional focus selected, and that focus can be anything from a joint, how it functions and relates to other aspects of the body, or the perception of what we see when we move as the eyes receive light from the space and we perceive others as we move. So although there is a set of shared processes in the method of generating learning across the classes covered by the umbrella term 'Release-based Technique', the practice is one of variation and exploration.

TECHNIQUES QUICK COMPARISON CHART

GRAHAM TECHNIQUE	CUNNINGHAM TECHNIQUE	RELEASE TECHNIQUE
Body		
Emphasis on initiation from the torso Many surfaces as support for weight	Articulation of the joints and spine with no hierarchy Feet as primary support	Integration of the body, use of sequencing along lines of connectivity
Action Content		
Opening Gesture Closing Jump Twist Transfer- Turn ence of Travel weight	Twist Jump Lean Transfer- Turn ence of Travel weight Gesture	Actions Closing seam- Transfer- lessly ence of intercon- weight nected: Twist Falling Turn Opening Travel
Kinespheric Space		
Spatial projection Large movements Locations in space	Body design Direct pathways 27 locations in space	Spatial progression Often no locational emphasis: three-dimensional flow
General Space		
Teacher establishes a front for class Travelling phrases cross the space	Teacher establishes a front for class Many changes in orientation for the dancer	No set front; constant changes in front Use of circles Relationship to partner
Dynamics		
Strong Varying degrees of bound flow Direct	Time Space Weight	Free flow Weight
Relationships		
Body centre to peripheries Energy out to the viewer and beyond them	Energy in the body equalized in all directions Viewer as active observer Arbitrary combinations and variations	Sequential relationships in the body Equality of viewer and performer

CONTRIBUTORS

Will Aitchinson: Will trained at the London Contemporary Dance School, where he gained his BA Hons in Contemporary Dance. He then went on to become a member of Transitions Dance Company at Trinity Laban Conservatoire of Music and Dance. Will performed in Matthew Bourne's *Swan Lake*, completing two international tours, a UK tour and a Sadler's Wells season. Since then Will has taught at graduate and undergraduate level, as well as many youth and community projects, and more recently at Arts Educational Schools, London, and as the Lead Teacher for the Centre for Advanced Training at Trinity Laban Conservatoire of Music and Dance. He is currently the Programme Leader for Contemporary Dance Foundation Programmes at Trinity Laban. Will co-founded his own company, called Anecdotal Evidence, in 2013.

Stephen Berkley-White: Stephen comes from Wiltshire and began his dance training at Thamesdown Dance Studios in Swindon, before going to Rambert Ballet School in London, as well as intensives at Merce Cunningham studios in New York. He was co-founder and choreographer of Triptych Dance Company, and was a joint winner of the Cosmopolitan/ C&A Dance Prize; he also won their inaugural choreography prize. He has performed with David Massingham Dance, Lloyd Newson for English National Opera, Diversions Dance Company (now Dance Company Wales), Wayne McGregor's Random Dance, Mark Bruce Company, and Matthew Bourne's *Swan Lake* and the creating cast of his production of *The Car Man*. In 2005 Stephen studied Photography at London College of Communication, and still works as a photographer and video artist today.

Rachel Burn: Rachel trained at Middlesex University and the Cunningham School in New York. She has taught at, and received commissions from Surrey, Middlesex and Lincoln universities, and the Attakkalari Centre for Movement Arts, Bangalore. She currently teaches at Trinity Laban. Rachel has made and shared her own explorative work at UK festivals, collaborating with musicians and film-makers. She has worked with Lithuanian physical theatre director Leva Kuniskis, Berlin-based film artist Grace Schwindt, interactive game-playing company The People Pile, and enjoyed several of Willi Dorners' *Bodies in Urban Spaces*. In 2014 she gave a TEDx talk for London Business School, introducing the idea of the body as a thinking and communicating form.

Marina Collard: Marina is a choreographer, independent dance artist and teacher. She works in collaboration with artists such as film-maker Tom Paine and composer Paul Newland. Choreographic commissions include *Ether*, at the Southbank Centre, London, with Graham Fitkin; a Tripspace commission in collaboration with the Hayward Gallery, where she collaborated with dance artist Kate Johnson; and the summer season at the Clore Studio, Royal Opera House, London, among others. Marina is working with dance artist Henrietta Hale on the creation of *Dream Clean – Clean Dream*, a multi-screen video installation. *On disturbance, instability and being here* is her most recent project, which had its initial phase of research at the Gati Dance Forum in Delhi, India.

Marina has been sent by the British Council to teach in India, Russia and Canada. She has been on the faculty at Trinity Laban and London Contemporary Dance School, and is a guest lecturer for MA Performance Practice (Dance) at Ambedkar University Delhi, India. She has contributed to programmes at Northern School of Contemporary Dance, UK; Central Saint Martin's (Design for Dance Module), UK; the Centre National de Dance Contemporaine, France; and the Attakkalari Centre for Movement Arts, India. As a performer, Marina has worked with ceramicist Claire Twomey, Florence Peake, the *Dog Kennel Hill* project, Joe Moran, Carol Brown Dances, the Candoco Dance Company, and Carolyn Roy, among others. Marina qualified as a biodynamic craniosacral practitioner in 2010 from CTET.

Jamieson Dryburgh: Jamieson is a lecturer at Trinity Laban Conservatoire of Music and Dance, specializing in Release-based Contemporary Dance Technique, dance pedagogy and participatory dance practice. He has danced for internationally renowned choreographers and companies including Candoco, Yolanda Snaith Theatre dance, Physical Recall, H2dane, Ben Wright, First Person, Yelp! (Greece), Charleroi/dances (Belgium), Tandem Cie (Belgium), among others. He was artistic director of Shift (integrated dance company @ The Place) for over seven years. Jamieson co-delivers dance within the social inclusion programme of Micro Rainbow International, who support LGBT+ refugees and asylum seekers. Currently, Jamieson is completing his PhD in Dance Pedagogy at Middlesex University. He has published peer-reviewed research in *Research in Dance Education* (co-authored with Louise Jackson), *Dance and Somatic Practices* and the *Journal of Dance Education*. He is a fellow of the Higher Education Academy, a board member of DanceHE, and Clore Leader.

Geneviève Grady: Geneviève is an independent dancer, choreographer and teacher on the BA (Hons) Contemporary Dance programme at Trinity Laban Conservatoire for Music and Dance. She has performed throughout Canada, the US and Europe, including aerial, film, site-specific projects, fusion and classical roles with Menaka Thakkar and Ritmo Flamenco, and three solos by choreographer Deborah Hay. She has a Masters in Choreography from Trinity Laban.

Tina Krasevec: Tina studied Sociology and Philosophy at the university in Slovenia before pursuing her passion for contemporary dance by studying at The London Contemporary Dance School, where she graduated with a BA in 1998. Tina has worked with various choreographers – Robert North, Sue MacLennan, Charles Linehan, Thomas Small and Duncan MacFarland, amongst others – whilst also furthering her professional training with a MSc Dance Science degree from Trinity Laban (2007–08), and more recently a Specialist Diploma in Choreological Studies (2013–16). Tina is currently a contemporary dance technique lecturer at Trinity Laban and Bird College.

Henry Montes: Henry is a freelance dance maker, performer and teacher. He has performed for many independent choreographers and companies in New York and Europe, including Susanne Linke, Reinhild Hoffmann, Keely Garfield, Kirstie Simson, KJ Holmes, Gaby Agis, Charles Linehan, Kate Brown, Rosemary Butcher, the Jonathan Burrows Group and Siobhan Davies Dance, and was awarded the 2003 Critics Circle National Dance Award for Outstanding Male Artist. He continues to study yoga and the Alexander Technique, and is a registered craniosacral therapist.

Alice Sara: Alice has performed with the Seven Sisters Group, including as a performer and choreographic assistant for their project *Like a Fish Out of Water*, created in partnership with the English National Ballet. She has recently performed with Lizzi Kew-Ross & Co, and has a long collaboration with the film-maker/choreographer Deborah Tiso, for whom she has performed in many films and multi-media projects. She took part in the Solo Commissioning Project with Deborah Hay, adapting and performing the solo *NEWS* in various festivals and venues. She has also worked as a performer with choreographers including Tom Dale, Cathy Seago, Maresa Von Stockert and Andreja Rausch. She has been teaching Release-based Technique, and creative and performance components at Trinity Laban Conservatoire for Music and Dance for over ten years, while continuing to teach, create and perform independently.

Ellen Van Schuylenburch: Ellen was born in Amsterdam and trained at the Rotterdam Dance Academy (now Codarts University of the Arts). She started attending classes at the Cunningham Studios in 1974. She danced with Rotterdam Werkcentrum Dans, and joined Nederlands Dans Theater 2 at the age of twenty-one. In New York she performed with experimental and post-Modern choreographers including Bill T. Jones and Arnie Zane, David Gordon, Albert Reid, Jim Self, Ton Simons and Karole Armitage. She became a founder member of Michael Clark Company, performing many works, and has been the assistant to Michael Clark and rehearsal director for Richard Alston Dance Company and Russell Maliphant Dance Company. She was Michael Clark Company's Special Projects and Artistic Documentation Officer, and set up Clark's archive. She performed in the works of artists Tino Sehgal, Alexis Blake and Nina Beier. She is a company teacher for Rambert Dance, Wayne McGregor's Random Dance, and the Michael Clark Company, and is a dance tutor and academic tutor at Trinity Laban Conservatoire for Music and Dance.

Daniel Squire: Daniel was born in Halifax, UK. He studied dance at White Lodge and at the Rambert School. He worked for many years as a member of the Merce Cunningham Dance Company, performing around the world. He has also performed in the work of John Kelly, John Scott, Paulina Olowska, Kimberly Bartosik and others. In 2013–14 he was curator for the dance programme for the exhibit *Dancing Around the Bride: Cage, Cunningham, Johns, Rauschenberg and Duchamp* at the Philadelphia Museum of Art, for which he worked closely with artist Philippe Parreno. He is on faculty at Trinity Laban Conservatoire of Music and Dance. In 2019 he staged *Night of 100 Solos: A Centennial Event* at the Barbican in London, on the occasion of Merce Cunningham's 100th birthday.

Sarah Sulemanji: Sarah is a lecturer in dance technique at Middlesex University, teaching technique and repertoire across the undergraduate courses. Sarah completed her professional training at The Martha Graham School of Contemporary Dance in New York in 2010, and continues to utilize Graham-based methods of technique training as a basis for her teaching practice. Sarah holds a first-class honours degree in Dance Performance, an MA in Professional Practice Dance Technique Pedagogy, and a Post Graduate Certificate in Higher Education, and has performed professionally in both the US and the UK. She has worked closely with Anne Donnelly throughout her time at Middlesex University, restaging and rehearsal-directing the work of Robert Cohan. She has also demonstrated for workshops and classes held by Martha Graham company members and the faculty from the Martha Graham School.

Rahel Vonmoos: Rahel is a Swiss/British independent dance maker, performer and lecturer. She has created a substantial body of work, presented in theatres, galleries and site-specific places in Europe and the USA, also at the Hayward Gallery, Dance Umbrella and the Spring Loaded Festival in London. Rahel has worked in collaborative contexts, amongst others, with dancer/choreographer Wally Cardona (NY), film-maker Ruth Schlaepfer (CH); and was commissioned by Tanzhaus ZH, Joyce SoHo (NY) and OiOiOi Project (N/UK, 2019). She worked as a dancer, amongst others, with Rosemary Butcher, Iztok Kovac (for film), Philippe Gehmacher and Charles Linehan, and in Switzerland with Cie Pool, Cie Molteni and Philippe Saire. Rahel is a certified Body-Mind Centering practitioner, and holds an MA in Arts: The Body in Performance. She teaches dance, improvization and performance practice for different organizations internationally, and is a guest lecturer at Trinity Laban Conservatoire for Music and Dance, BA and MA.

David Waring: David graduated from the Laban Centre for Movement and Dance in 1987 and has performed and choreographed with a range of artists including Ricochet Dance Company, Extemporary Dance Theatre Company, Motionhouse, Walker Dance, Adventures in Motion Pictures, The Featherstonehaughs and his group, fishpool (co-directed with Gaynor Coward). From 2000 to 2002 David was a participant and assistant director at Performing Arts Lab (PAL), and since 2002 has been the artistic director of Transitions Dance Company and Co-Programme Leader of the MA/MFA Dance Performance programme at Trinity Laban. Recent performance and choreographic work include Kate Brown's *and yet…*, Athina Vahla's *Listening Post*, and his own solo *hustler* at the Capital Nights festival in Liverpool, supported by Merseyside Dance Initiative and Homotopia. *hustler #2* premièred in Big Dance 2010, supported by Greenwich Dance, and was also part of Greenwich and Docklands International Festival 2011. He has studied Zero Balancing and has an MSc Mindfulness degree.

GLOSSARY

anatomy Our bodily structure.

autonomy Being self-governed and self-responsible, taking control of oneself and one's life.

archetypal Strong examples of particular types of persons. *The Cambridge Dictionary* defines this as 'a typical example of something, or the original model of something from which others are copied'

biomechanics How the body works as a whole unit in response to forces acting within and upon it.

Body-Mind Centering A patented system of movement therapy created by Bonnie Bainbridge Cohen.

developmental patterns 'Developmental progression: basic body connections are established through a stage specific developmental progression early in life. These basic connectivity patterns become integrated in the adult, and function as patterns of total body connectivity, which are then available for timely use and phrasing according to context.'[212]

exteroceptors Senses that bring us information about the external environment.

fascia Myofascia is a special kind of connective tissue in the body that exists in layers between muscles as well as connecting muscles into groups. Fascia is a continuous system that extends throughout the body that makes up our contours and holds us in place.[213]

interioceptors Senses that allow us to sense ourselves from the inside, through internal perception, so we feel our basic emotions such as hunger, we feel our relationship to gravity, and feel ourselves moving by sensing the positioning of our bones and the tones within our musculature.

kinesphere The three-dimensional spherical spatial field around us that emanates from our body centre and extends to the limit of our physical reach. We carry our kinesphere with us when we move, and it contains our spatial properties – our dimensions and planes.

physiology How our body functions.

proscenium arch theatre The most common type of theatre building in the 18th, 19th and 20th centuries. The arch at the front of the stage acts like a picture frame through which the action on stage can be seen from the auditorium. Most theatres built after the 1950s do not have a visible framing but the arrangement of the space in which the auditorium faces directly on to one side of the squared performance area is the same. This type of arrangement is sometimes referred to as the audience seeing the action through the invisible fourth wall of the stage.

reflect To think deeply and carefully.

self-reflective awareness The ability to think back and consider your actions and reactions in order to become more self-knowledgeable.

Skinner Releasing Technique (SRT) Skinner Releasing Technique is a somatic movement practice created by Joan Skinner that utilises hand-on partner studies and guided imagery to help people let go of habitual holding patterns and explore movement to support technical and creative movement practice.[214]

spatial planes The vertical or door plane (like standing within a door frame): a circle in space that connects the vertical and lateral dimensions. The sagittal or wheel plane (imagine a wheel rolling forward or backwards): a circle in space that connects the vertical and sagittal dimensions. The horizontal or table plane (horizontal to the floor like a table top): a circle in space that connects the sagittal and lateral dimensions.

tensegrity A property of a stable three-dimensional structure consisting of parts under tension that are together and touching, and parts that are under compression that are not touching. In bodily tensegrity the connective tissues or myofascia is continuous and interconnected as an overall system, and the bones are denser structures that are separated. This separation in maintained by the fluid within the joints that is excreted from the tissues surrounding the joint and relate the bones to each other across these separations, and in a relationship within the interconnected web of the body system.

REFERENCES

Chapter 1
1 Tina Krasevec, personal communication, 10 October 2017.

Chapter 2
2 Rachel Burn, personal communication, 28 March 2018.
3 Preston-Dunlop, 1979.
4 Preston-Dunlop, 1981.
5 Laban and Ullmann, 2011.
6 Jamieson Dryburgh, personal communication, 9 February 2018.
7 Rachel Burn, personal communication, 28 March 2018.
8 Tina Krasevec, personal communication, 10 October 2017.
9 Foster, 2007.
10 Rachel Burn, personal communication, 28 March 2018.
11 Stephen Berkeley White, personal communication, 21 November 2017.
12 Franklin 2003; Quin, Rafferty and Tomlinson 2015.
13 Following the work of Imgard Bartenieff (Hackney, 1998a).
14 Guest, 2005.
15 Watkins, 1999.
16 Hackney, 1998a; Watkins, 1999.
17 Watkins, 1999.
18 Watkins, 1999, p.16.
19 Myers, 2014a.
20 Feldenkrais, 1987, p.70.
21 Franklin, 2003.
22 David Waring, personal communication, 16 February 2018.
23 Hackney, 1998a.

Chapter 3
24 De Mille, 1991.
25 Simonari, 2012.
26 Brown, Mindlin and Woodford, 1998, p.50.
27 Brown et al., 1998.
28 Armitage, 1937/1966.
29 Helpern, 1999a.
30 Helpern, 1999a.
31 De Mille, 1991.
32 Helpern, 1999a.
33 Tracy, 1997, p.13.
34 Geneviève Grady, personal communication, 16 January 2019.

35 Sarah Sulemanji, personal communication, 13 March 2019.
36 Geneviève Grady, personal communication, 16 January 2019.
37 De Mille, 1991.
38 Geneviève Grady, personal communication, 16 January 2019.
39 S. Sulemanji, personal communication, 13 March 2019.
40 Helpern, 1999a, p.13.
41 G. Grady, personal communication, 16 January 2019.
42 Myers, 2014b.
43 Hackney, 1998b.
44 S. Sulemanji, personal communication, 13 March 2019.
45 De Mille, 1991.
46 Geneviève Grady, personal communication, 16 January 2019.
47 S. Sulemanji, personal communication, 13 March 2019.
48 De Mille, 1991.
49 Sarah Sulemanji, personal communication, 13 March 2019.
50 Preston-Dunlop, 1981.
51 Geneviève Grady, personal communication, 16 January 2019.
52 Geneviève Grady, personal communication, 16 January 2019.
53 Guest, 2005.
54 Geneviève Grady, personal communication, 16 January 2019.
55 Preston-Dunlop, 1978.
56 Armitage, 1937/1966.
57 Armitage, 1937/1966.
58 Schleip, Baker and Avison, 2015a.
59 Sarah Sulemanji, personal communication, 13 March 2019.
60 Laban and Ullmann, 1960.
61 Geneviève Grady, personal communication, 16 January 2019.
62 Helpern, 1999a, p.13.
63 Armitage, 1937/1966.
64 Laban and Ullmann, 1960.
65 Laban and Ullmann, 1960.
66 Fettes, Malmgren and Laban, 2015.
67 De Mille, 1991.
68 Laban and Ullmann, 1960.
69 Fettes et al., 2015, p.225.
70 Laban and Ullmann, 1960.
71 Fettes et al., 2015, p.219.

72 Helpern, 1999b.
73 Armitage, 1937/1966.
74 Geneviève Grady, personal communication, 19 February 2018.
75 Geneviève Grady, personal communication, 19 February 2018.
76 Geneviève Grady, personal communication, 19 February 2018.
77 Geneviève Grady, 19 February 2018.
78 Geneviève Grady, personal communication, 16 January 2019.
79 Sarah Sulemanji, personal communication, 13 March 2019.

Chapter 4
80 Jowitt 1985.
81 Banes, Acocella and Garafola, 2007.
82 Cunningham and Lesschaeve, 1985.
83 Croce, 1978.
84 Cunningham and Lesschaeve, 1985.
85 Walker Art Center, 2009.
86 Banes, Harris, Acocella and Garafola, 2007.
87 Banes et al., 2007.
88 Banes et al., 2007.
89 Banes et al., 2007.
90 Cunningham and Lesschaeve, 1985.
91 Ellen Van Schuylenburch, personal communication, 8 December 2017.
92 Bremser, 1999.
93 Cunningham and Lesschaeve, 1985.
94 Stephen Berkeley White, personal communication, 21 November 2017.
95 Cunningham and Lesschaeve, 1985.
96 William Aitchison, personal communication, 15 June 2018.
97 Rachel Burn, personal communication, 28 March 2018.
98 Ellen Van Schuylenburch, personal communication, 8 December 2017.
99 Stephen Berkeley White, personal communication, 21 November 2017.
100 Rachel Burn, personal communication, 28 March 2018.
101 Preston-Dunlop, 1981.
102 Cunningham and Lesschaeve, 1991.
103 Preston-Dunlop, 1998.
104 Preston-Dunlop, 1979.
105 Rachel Burn, personal communication, 28 March 2018.
106 Ellen Van Schuylenburch, personal

communication, 8 Dec 2017.
107 Rachel Burn, personal communication, 28 March 2018.
108 Kostelanetz, 1992.
109 Ellen Van Schuylenburch, personal communication, 8 December 2017.
110 Cunningham, Lesschaeve 1991.
111 Preston-Dunlop, 1979.
112 Daniel Squire, personal communication, 6 October 2017.
113 Laban and Ullmann, 1960.
114 Stephen Berkeley White, personal communication, 21 November 2017.
115 Rachel Burn, personal communication, 28 March 2018.
116 S. Berkeley White, personal communication, 21 November 2017.
117 Laban and Lawrence, 1947; Laban and Ullmann, 1960.
118 Jowitt, 1985.
119 Cunningham and Lesschaeve, 1985.
120 Laban and Lawrence, 1947.
121 Daniel Squire, personal communication, 6 October 2017.
122 Jowitt, 1985.
123 Cunningham and Lesschaeve, 1985.
124 Stephen Berkeley White, personal communication, 21 November 2017.
125 Cunningham and Lesschaeve, 1985.
126 Ellen Van Schuylenburch, personal communication, 8 December 2017.
127 Croce 1978.
128 Rachel Burn, personal communication, 28 March 2018.
129 Stephen Berkeley White, personal communication, 21 November 2017.
130 Kostelanetz, 1992.
131 Stephen Berkeley White, personal communication, 21 November 2017.
132 Rachel Burn, personal communication, 28 March 2018.
133 Ellen Van Schuylenburch, personal communication, 8 December 2017.
134 Daniel Squire, personal communication, 6 October 2017.
135 (Jowitt, 1985).
136 Cunningham and Lesschaeve, 1985.
137 Cunningham and Lesschaeve, 1985.
138 Daniel Squire, personal communication, 6 October 2017.
139 Ellen Van Schuylenburch, personal communication, 8 December 2017.
140 Daniel Squire, personal communication, 6 October 2017.
141 Stephen Berkeley White, personal communication, 21 November 2017.
142 William Aitchison, personal communication, 15 June 2018.

143 Rachel Burn, personal communication, 28 March 2018.
144 Rachel Burn, personal communication, 28 March 2018.
145 Daniel Squire, personal communication, 6 October 2017.
146 Stephen Berkeley White, personal communication, 21 November 2017.
147 William Aitchison, personal communication, 15 June 2018.
148 Daniel Squire, personal communication, 6 October 2017.

Chapter 5
149 Richterich, 1998; Whatley, Garrett Brown and Alexander, 2015.
150 Kovarova and Miranda, 2006.
151 Foster, 2007.
152 Johnson, 1995.
153 Johnson, 1995.
154 Richterich, 1998.
155 Johnson, 1995.
156 Schleip et al., 2015a.
157 Kovarova and Miranda, 2006.
158 Hanna, 1988.
159 Kovarova and Miranda, 2006.
160 Kovarova and Miranda, 2006.
161 Henry Montes, personal communication, 8 February 2017.
162 Johnson, 1995.
163 Alice Sara, personal communication, 3 October 2017.
164 Tandon et al., n.d.
165 Salvitti, 2016.
166 Whatley et al., 2015.
167 Hargreaves et al., 2003, p.7.
168 Marina Collard, personal communication, 2 October 2018.
169 David Waring, personal communication, 16 February 2018.
170 Jamieson Dryburgh, personal communication, 9 February 2018.
171 Marina Collard, personal communication, 2 October 2018.
172 Henry Montes, personal communication, 2 February 2017.
173 Jamieson Dryburgh, personal communication, 9 February 2018.
174 Tina Krasevec, personal communication, 10 October 2017.
175 Jamieson Dryburgh, personal communication, 9 February 2018.
176 Rahel Vonmoos, personal communication, 7 February 2018.
177 Batson and Wilson, 2014.
178 David Waring, personal communication, 16 February 2018.
179 David Waring, personal communica-

tion, 16 February 2018.
180 Henry Montes, personal communication, 8 February 2017.
181 Hackney, 1998b.
182 Marina Collard, personal communication, 2 October 2018.
183 Henry Montes, personal communication, 8 February 2017.
184 Henry Montes, personal communication, 8 February 2017.
185 David Waring, personal communication, 16 February 2018.
186 Kovarova and Miranda, 2006.
187 Hackney, 1998b.
188 Myers, 2014b.
189 Hackney, 1998b.
190 Cohen, Nelson and Smith, 2012.
191 Alice Sara, personal communication 3 October 2017.
192 Marina Collard, personal communication, 2 October 2018.
193 Whatley et al., 2015.
194 Marina Collard, personal communication, 2 October 2018.
195 Nelson, 2013.
196 Jamieson Dryburgh, personal interview, 2018.
197 Marina Collard, personal communication, 2 October 2018.
198 Kovarova & Miranda, 2006.
199 Marina Collard, personal communication, 2 October 2018.
200 Marina Collard, personal communication, 2 October 2018.
201 Jamieson Dryburgh, personal communication, 9 February 2018.
202 Alice Sara, personal communication, 3 October 2017.
203 Hargreaves et al., 2003.
204 Marina Collard, personal communication, 2 October 2018.
205 Kovarova and Miranda, 2006.
206 Kovarova et al., 2006, p.18.
207 Rahel Vonmoos, personal communication, 7 February 2018.
208 Jamieson Dryburgh, personal communication, 9 February 2018.
209 David Waring, personal communication, 16 February 2018.
210 Alice Sara, personal communication, 3 October 2017.
211 Marina Collard, personal communication, 2 October 2018.
212 Hackney, 1998a.
213 Schleip, Baker and Avison, 2015b.
214 http://www.skinnerreleasing.com/aboutsrt.html.

BIBLIOGRAPHY

Armitage, M. (1966) *Martha Graham* (reprint of 1937 edition Articles by John Martin, Lincoln Kirstein, Evangeline Stokowski, Stark Young, Wallingford Riegger, Edith J. R. Isaacs, Roy Hargrave, James Johnson Sweeney, George Antheil, Margaret Lloyd, Louis Danz, and Martha Graham.). New York: Dance Horizons Inc. (Original work published 1937).

Banes, S., Acocella, J. R., and Garafola, L. (2007) *Before, between, and beyond: Three decades of dance writing* (A. Harris, ed.) Madison: University of Wisconsin Press.

Batson, G., & Wilson, M. (2014). *Body and mind in motion: dance and neuroscience in conversation*. Bristol Chicago: Intellect.

Bremser, M. (1999) *Fifty contemporary choreographers*. London; New York: Routledge.

Brown, J. M., Mindlin, N., and Woodford, C. H. (eds) (1998) *The vision of modern dance: In the words of its creators* (2nd ed.). London, England: Dance Books.

Cambridge Dictionary (n.d.). Retrieved 17 July 2019, from https://dictionary.cambridge.org/dictionary/english

Cohen, B. B., Nelson, L., and Smith, N. S. (2012) *Sensing, feeling, and action: the experiential anatomy of body-mind centering®* (third edition). Northampton, MA: Contact Editions.

Croce, A. (1978) *Afterimages*. London: Adam and Charles Black.

Cunningham, M., and Lesschaeve, J. (1985) *The dancer and the dance*. New York: Boyars.

De Mille, A. (1991) *Martha: the life and work of Martha Graham* (1st ed.) New York: Random House.

Feldenkrais, M. (1987) *Awareness through movement: health exercises for personal growth*. Harmondsworth: Penguin.

Fettes, C., Malmgren, Y., and Laban, R. von. (2015) *A peopled labyrinth: The histrionic sense: An analysis of the actor's craft: The Laban-Carpenter 'Theory of Movement Psychology' adapted and brought to completion by Yat Malmgren*. London, England: GFCA Publishing.

Foster, M. A. (2007) *Somatic patterning: How to improve posture and movement and ease pain*. Longmont, CO: EMS Press. (LAB 320 FOS).

Franklin, E. N. (2003) *Pelvic power: mind/body exercises for strength, flexibility, posture, and balance for men and women*. Highstown, NJ: Elysian Editions.

Guest, A. H. (2005) *Labanotation: the system of analyzing and recording movement* (4th ed., rev). New York: Routledge.

Hackney, P. (1998a) *Making connections: total body integration through Bartenieff fundamentals* (2. ed, digital printing). The Netherlands, Amsterdam, Gordon and Breach.

Hanna, T. (1988) *Somatics: reawakening the mind's control of movement, flexibility, and health*. Cambridge MA, Da Capo Press.

Hargreaves, M., Alexander, K., Fortin, S., Tandon, R., Bober, J. M., Skelton, R., Veropoulou, E. (2003) *New connectivity : somatic and creative practices in dance education*. Papers from the Laban research conference 19 July 2003. Presented at the London. London: Laban.

Helpern, A. J. (1999a) *Martha Graham*. New York: Routledge.

Johnson, D. H. (ed.) (1995) *Bone, breath and gesture: Practices of embodiment*. Berkeley, CA: North Atlantic Books. (LAB 338 JOH).

Jowitt, D. (1985) *The dance in mind: profiles and reviews 1976-83* (1st ed.). Boston: D.R. Godine.

Kostelanetz, R. (1992) *Merce Cunningham: dancing in space and time.* London: Dance Books.

Kovarova, M., Miranda, R., Austvoll, A., Bradley, K., Cohen, B. B., Bryan, H., Fernandes, C. (2006) *Laban and performing arts : proceedings of conference Bratislava* [6-8 October] Slovakia: Bratislava in Movement Association.

Laban, R., and Lawrence, F.C. (1947) *Effort.* London: Macdonald & Evans.

Laban, R. von, and Ullmann, L. (1960) *The mastery of movement* (2d ed., and enl). London: MacDonald & Evans.

Laban, R. von, & Ullmann, L. (2011) *The mastery of movement.* Alton: Dance books.

Martha Graham Dance Company (n.d.) *Martha Graham Dance Technique beginning level* [Youtube.com]. Retrieved 17 July 2019, from https://www.youtube.com/watch?v=cZ2tG5TPANA#action=share

Merce Cunningham Trust. (2013) MERCE CUNNINGHAM: MONDAYS WITH MERCE #1:TECHNIQUE. Retrieved from https://www.youtube.com/watch?v=q318rHkDDHo

Merce Cunningham Trust. (2016a). CUNNINGHAM TECHNIQUE® COMPANY CLASS 7.29.2009 (close view). Retrieved from https://www.youtube.com/watch?v=kjGlj189fdM

Merce Cunningham Trust (2016b) CUNNINGHAM TECHNIQUE® COMPANY CLASS 7.30.2009 (close view). Retrieved from https://www.youtube.com/watch?v=9Wtnl32uvM4

Myers, T. W. (2014a) *Anatomy trains: myofascial meridians for manual and movement therapists* (3rd ed.). Edinburgh: Elsevier.

Nelson, M. (2013) 'Polycentrism in contemporary dance', Journal of Dance & Somatic Practices, 5(2), 155–168. https://doi.org/10.1386/jasper.5.2.155_1

Preston-Dunlop, V. (1978) *Investigation into the spontaneous occurance of fragments of choreutic forms in choreographed dance works.* London Goldsmiths College.

Preston-Dunlop, V. (1979) *Dance is a language isn't it?* London: Laban Centre for Movement and Dance.

Preston-Dunlop, V. (1981) *Nature of the Embodiment of Choreutic units in Contemporary Choreography*: (unpublished thesis) Laban, London.

Preston-Dunlop, V. (1998) *Looking at dances : a choreological perspective on choreography.* UK Verve.

Richterich, E. (1998) *Releasing What?: An analysis of the history and conceptual basis of Release Technique* (unpublished thesis). Laban, London, England.

Salvitti, S.M. (2016) 'Considering Klein Technique: A core stability alternative for contemporary dance education' Journal of Dance and Somatic Practices, Volume 8 (Number 2).

Schleip, R., Baker, A., and Avison, J. (eds) (2015a) *Fascia in sport and movement.* Edinburgh: Handspring Publishing.

Simonari, R. (2012) 'Dead or alive?': Martha Graham's legacy twenty years after she passed away. Ballet Dance Magazine, (Jan 2012). Retrieved from http://www.ballet-dance.com/201201/Graham-Jan2012.html

Tandon, R., Bober, J. M., Skelton, R., Chappell, K., Nunes, A., Timmons, W., and Veropoulou, E. (n.d.) *New connectivity: Somatic and creative practices in dance education: Papers from the Laban Research Conference 19 July 2003* (M. Hargreaves, G. Dutton and E. Gilbert, eds) London, England: Laban.

Tracy, R. (1997) *Goddess: Martha Graham's dancers remember* (1st Limelight ed.) New York: Limelight Editions.

Walker Art Center. (2009) *Chance Conversations: An Interview with Merce Cunningham and John Cage.* Retrieved from https://www.youtube.com/watch?v=ZNGpjXZovgk

Watkins, J. (1999) *Structure and function of the musculoskeletal system.* Champaign, IL: Human Kinetics.

Whatley, S., Garrett Brown, N., and Alexander, K. (2015) *Attending to Movement: somatic perspectives on living in this world.* Axminster, England: Triarchy Press.

INDEX